Reading The Water:
A Life Spent Fishing

'A very enjoyable read ... Fishermen all over the world will like this book.'
Jack Charlton

'*Reading the Water* is a well-crafted, informative and highly enjoyable book that anglers and non-anglers alike will enjoy. Darryl's love of the pursuit of a wide variety of fish, from Perch to Giant Tuna, is equalled by his respect for each of the species and his concern for the preservation of the natural habitat so vital to their survival ... This is a most worthwhile book by one who is an accomplished writer and a consummate fisherman.'
General John de Chastelain

'Darryl writes fine descriptions of the highs and lows of making fishing programmes for television – the passion is evident and the good days and bad days are eloquently described. I would highly recommend this book for anglers of all disciplines. I lived every page, and, best of all, his enthusiasm shines through. I'd share a day with him anytime.
I *know* you'll enjoy this book as much as I did.'
Paul Young (Presenter, 'Hooked on Fishing')

'A fine book ... No recent angling writer has so vividly evoked the joys and angst of pursuing wild fish in Ireland as Darryl Grimason. Curl up with this splendid book on a cold winter's evening and join him, with salt spray in your face off Kenbane Head and East Ferry or with a gentle breeze wafting down from the Maamturks, as he raises Melvin sonaghan and Corrib browns to his fly, hunts elusive Ferox and battles with blue sharks and other leviathans of the deep.'
Jonathan Bardon

Darryl Grimason is a journalist with BBC Northern Ireland and has presented two television series on fishing, *Coast to Coast* and *Big Six*.

Reading the Water
A Life Spent Fishing

Darryl Grimason

ILLUSTRATIONS by
TIM STAMPTON

THE O'BRIEN PRESS
DUBLIN

First published 2005 by The O'Brien Press Ltd,
20 Victoria Road, Dublin 6, Ireland.
Tel: +353 1 4923333; Fax: +353 1 4922777
E-mail: books@obrien.ie
Website: www.obrien.ie

ISBN: 0-86278-914-1

British Library Cataloguing-in-Publication Data
A catalogue record for this title is available from the British Library

1 2 3 4 5 6
04 05 06 07 08 09

Editing, typesetting, layout and design: The O'Brien Press Ltd
Illustrations: Tim Stampton

Picture Credits:
Front Cover: Irish Image Collection
Front Flap: Alan Hill
Back Cover: Steve Wilson
Back Flap, top: Alan Hill; bottom: Roger Ford-Hutchinson

Printing: Creative Print & Design, Wales

Dedication

For Karen, Kirsten and Erin

ACKNOWLEDGEMENTS

This is a short list of those who helped me with this book and whom I must acknowledge. I particularly want to thank Helene, Jane, Averil and Sheelagh, daughters of my late 'Uncle' Holt, for their kindness and memories.

My friend Harry Hamilton deserves special mention too. For your support, warmth and encouragement when self-doubt kicked in, thanks H.

I am grateful to my employer, BBC Northern Ireland, for allowing me to write about my television exploits.

I have also drawn on research I did for the fishing series, *Coast to Coast* and *Big Six*.

Collective thanks are due to the very many experts and anglers who so generously shared their knowledge with me.

Finally, a big thank you to everyone I've ever fished with, because that positive experience has informed this book too.

'To see a World in a Grain of Sand
And a Heaven in a Wild Flower,
Hold Infinity in the palm of your hand
And Eternity in an hour.'

(William Blake, *Auguries of Innocence*)

CONTENTS

BEGINNINGS

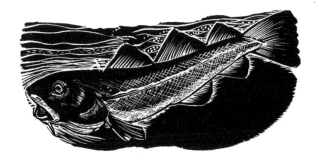

Rummaging about in the dark, nearly forgotten corners of my mind, a figure begins to appear in the haze. Little by little the shape of the far distant past begins to suggest itself. I'm searching for the start of my lifelong love affair with fishing.

Slowly, the figure moves from the back to the front of my mind. It's as if the fog of thirty five years is clearing. And there he is: Holt McKenzie – my 'Uncle' Holt.

I haven't thought about him for so long that the memory is like a dream.

Holt McKenzie: what a fabulous name! It sounds like it could have been made up, but he was the real deal, a genuine huntin', shootin', fishin' gentleman. The name suited him well.

When I was about five years old, he bought me my first fishing rod. That day he also took me on my first fishing trip – I've never received more important gifts.

Uncle Holt was a friend of my father's. I loved him and knew he adored me. It's the sort of thing children know with absolute certainty without needing to be told. His warmth and kind looks said it all.

I remember him as tall, dark and handsome, a man's man who could charm the birds out of the trees. He was larger than life. To me, a scrawny kid, barely standing above his knee, he was a giant.

At this distance, my picture of him is at the same time vivid and imprecise. I have an inkling of a loose-limbed athletic frame, dark, hooded eyes and a beaming smile. It was the late sixties – and his hair, going grey at the temples, was slicked back with Brylcreem.

The nose was aquiline with a little bump on the bridge. It was a permanent reminder of a collision with the back of a parked Morris Minor car. He'd cycled into it in the pitch black of the night. And when he got home, he washed away the blood at the kitchen sink and squeezed the broken cartilage back into place with a loud click. Uncle Holt was as hard as nails.

He looked big and strong and I so much wanted to be like him. Occasionally he'd turn up on horseback at the doorstep of our council house in Lurgan. He would breeze into view, a vision in jodhpurs, black riding boots, tweed jacket and a hard black hat. In the middle of a working class housing estate, all the kids would run alongside this almost surreal apparition.

The chorus of 'Mister, give us a ride on your horse, ah go on!' was punctuated by the clip clopping of his huge dapple-grey horse. It must have been an odd sight. To me, it seemed the most natural thing in the world. He'd scoop my skinny frame up in his arms and let me sit on his lap. There, enveloped in a cloud of Old Spice aftershave and the faint whiff of tobacco, I'd hold the reins and pretend I was John Wayne. It felt like I was on top of the world, picked out, special.

I was the third of four children reared in an end-of-terrace house on a tight budget. Seventeen Colban Crescent in Lurgan was a cold space. In winter the condensation froze on the inside of the metal-framed bedroom windows. Away from the small semi-circle of heat cast out by the fire in the living room there was no warmth. This was long before we learned about the comfort of radiators and central heating.

Our only warmth upstairs came from a paraffin heater, which thawed the night air in the bedrooms. A dome of wire netting acted as a filament. It glowed dark red at the highest point and bright orange at the rim where it touched the blue and yellow flames. It would be wheeled precariously across the landing from my sisters' room onto the linoleum of the bedroom my brother and I shared. It cast a faint light and snored quietly as it pumped heat and an oily scent around the room.

Both my parents did their best. They worked hard but they were never able to provide us with any luxuries

There were nights when scrambled egg was the main meal – sometimes banana sandwiches. I was forever in hand-me-down clothes, as was my younger sister.

Uncle Holt couldn't have been further removed from that life. He looked like he'd just stepped off a Hollywood set when he'd make an entrance on his horse. There was a touch of glamour, of romance, about him.

He was into fox hunting and that brought him, and on one memorable occasion me, into contact with the top people. It's a bizarre recollection, but I distinctly remember talking to the then Prime Minister of Northern Ireland, Brian Faulkner.

He was drinking sherry from a tiny glass while mounted on a huge horse when my Uncle Holt took me by the hand and led me to him. The man was wearing the traditional red jacket, white riding britches and shiny black knee-length boots.

He was surrounded by the well-to-do members of the Iveagh Harriers, all kitted out in the same uniform. There was noise and chatter. Everyone was excited at the promise of the chase and a day in the saddle. The metal shoes of the horses grated and rang on the rippled concrete of a farmyard somewhere. I was led through the confusion, past the weaving, sniffing pack of foxhounds, and taken to meet the guest of honour.

Uncle Holt picked me up and plonked me down astride the Prime Minister's horse. I was sitting right in front of him. The politician with the silver, slicked back hair shook my hand and told me to call him Brian, which I did. I was allowed a sip of his sherry and afterwards told everyone that the Prime Minister was my friend.

I think my father, Uncle Holt and myself spent the afternoon chasing the hunt in our Hillman Hunter car.

Not all Uncle Holt's friends were top drawer. Black Barney was a case in point. He'd regularly bump into the scruffy farmer on the shores of Lough Erne, under the Cliffs of Magho. According to Uncle Holt, Black Barney was a great character who lived in a small cottage on the road to Ballyshannon.

He was a bachelor and lived alone. Long before fast food made it across the Atlantic, he had invented his 'Fermanagh slice.' He'd make a huge cauldron of porridge once a week, a delicacy to which he gave a delicious title: he called it his 'stirabout'. It was poured, cement-like, into the bottom drawer of his dressing table where it cooled and solidified. A wedge was cut every morning and eaten cold. Strangely, it never caught on.

And so it went. Uncle Holt would dip in and out of my early life at irregular intervals, telling tall tales and bearing gifts. He'd sometimes appear with wood pigeons shot from behind straw bales on the stubble fields of County Down. Once they were handed over to me at the front door in a cardboard shoebox. The grey-blue birds with bloody beaks were softly layered, head to tail, just like sardines.

He'd also turn up with wild ducks shot from a stone hide on the shores of Lough Neagh on a sharp, icy morning, just before Christmas.

He'd tell me all about his adventures with the gun and

the rod and promise that when I was older I could come too. He did ask my mother if she'd let me take a day off primary school in order to go shooting with him. Mum did the responsible thing and said no – all these years later I wish she'd said yes.

There are some opportunities that are too good to be missed. Things and people that colour your life until you die – I'm sorry I didn't get to know him better.

I was still a child, only eight years old, when he was killed. It was a Sunday afternoon and he was training a young horse, an everyday event for the big man. He regularly schooled his brother's horses so they could be sold on for the hunt.

But this day in September 1971, the novice horse refused the jump. The hindquarters slid forward under its barrel body and the big animal fell on Uncle Holt. My parents didn't tell me about it at the time, they wanted to protect me from the grief. But I thought of him again years later when the news bulletins announced that his friend, and mine, Brian Faulkner had been killed in a riding accident.

Later still my Mum told me Uncle Holt had wanted to adopt me, and had actually asked my parents if they'd let me go. He was married and had four girls of his own but in me he saw the son he'd never have. I sort of understood that without needing to be told. I didn't know then what I'd lost. But I do now.

Through Uncle Holt, I first gained a sense of a life that's bigger and bolder than the everyday. On the riverbank, absorbed in stalking a fish, the predictability of a humdrum existence fades to nothing. On the open lough, among the waves and searching for fish there is a voice that soothes the soul and fills the heart.

This is the time and the place where life and nature merge, where you can be a speck of humanity in a vast landscape. There are no straight lines, no considerations beyond the here and now and the hunt.

Out there, our time has no meaning beyond the moment, the days slide by in a flash and the success of finding and hooking a trout makes the heart beat faster and the mind race. I am forever five years old when I'm in that place; forever the impressionable child who can shed the cares of age and experience and exist in the joy of just being alive.

It was the same for Uncle Holt. Every weekend in the summer he would make the long drive down to Fermanagh in the hope that the trout would be up and feeding on the mayfly.

I can only imagine him with his Hardy 'Knockabout' rod, casting from a wooden boat. Four decades apart we tie on the same Golden Olive Bumble pattern, pull it through the same water and wait with the same excitement for the same trout to seize it.

The place is the same too, but there is no physical trace of him, me or any of the other men who hunt this wilderness after we leave. It's a humbling thought, our stories are written only on the water. This landscape has no memory.

It's odd that I haven't thought about Uncle Holt for such a long time when in fact he's been with me all along.

When I first started fly fishing about fifteen years ago I thought of him. I wished he were still around to share the passion, to guide, advise and tutor. I knew he'd be so proud of me, I wanted his approval.

Without him, it was left to my brother-in-law Andy Holden to teach me the rudiments of casting. I dug out my first fly fishing rod, a dreadful brush shaft of a thing. I'd bought it when I was about eleven years old in the Golden Arrow sports shop in Carnegie Street, opposite the library in Lurgan.

I'd tried to master the noble art and failed miserably. I had been able to cast a line but had not the faintest idea what flies to use and in which situation, so I failed to catch anything. I gave it up as a bad job.

Andy took me to the River Bann near Banbridge and I caught every tree close enough to be hooked. But little by little, with his help I began to catch trout, at first under the surface on wet flies.

When I mastered catching river trout on the dry fly there was no looking back. I had found my Nirvana. That was the start of an obsession that floods my waking thoughts during the game fishing season and at odd moments in the winter. Uncle Holt would have totally understood.

The first time I went salmon fishing to Donegal with friends I had a sense of him. Many years earlier, I remember carrying a salmon into our house that he'd caught on the fly in the River Finn. I held it by the baling twine looped through its gills and upturned lower jaw. Its black tail trailed the shiny linoleum on the kitchen floor. The broad silver-blue flanks coated my jumper with slime.

It was laid out on the red formica-topped table and everyone gathered around to see it – another gift to the family from a world beyond our knowledge or understanding. I was in awe that this man was so gifted that he could pluck such a monster from the river.

He sowed the seeds of my great passion for fishing on a chance encounter one summer's day. We bumped into him by accident in Newcastle in County Down half a lifetime ago.

I think the family was on a day-trip to the seaside resort. Slieve Donard loomed large over the main street as it does today, and there stood Uncle Holt. He was with friends, leaning over the bridge above the River Shimna, watching it slide by, shallow and clear.

I imagine him peering through the surface reflections for a glimpse of a seat trout or salmon, waiting for that adrenalin spike of recognition, in exactly the same way I do now.

There's something about bridges that attracts fishers. There are the men with an ice cream cone in one hand and the other shielding the eyes like a peaked cap, who have to be pulled away by wives, partners or children. There's never a chance of fulfilling that fishing dream on those dutiful days, but it still doesn't stop us looking.

Anyway, there he stood killing time until the tide turned and the adventure could begin. My brother Stephen was there. He already had a fishing rod. It was six foot, solid green fibreglass and had dark green whippings. Time had been set aside for him to fish from the rocks. But it seemed there was room on Uncle Holt's boat for one more.

He wanted to take me and the fact that I didn't own a rod was not a problem. He was intent on taking me 'deep sea' fishing. So we went into a shop selling plastic buckets and spades, striped canvas windbreaks with their sowed-in wooden poles and a thousand and one other seaside 'necessities'. At the very back of this Aladdin's cave was a collection of cheap fishing tackle.

Uncle Holt expertly extracted a seven-foot spinning outfit from the forest of rods poking out of a big container. I was particularly delighted because now I had a bigger rod than my eleven-year-old brother.

The Black Prince reel was quickly spooled with strong nylon. It was rainbow line, a two-tone brown and green monofiliment that I've never seen since.

So there I was, back on the main street, the proud owner of a brand new fishing outfit, fully equipped for that day and the lifetime to follow.

I waved goodbye to my brother as we eased out of the harbour in a small open boat. The air stood still and the sea glistened flat and oily. Stephen was already fishing from the rocks, his legs crossed on the buff granite breakwater. He stared at his rod tip, blinking in the harsh sunlight. He had a determined look about him.

We headed for Bloody Bridge, where the Mountains of Mourne sweep down to the sea. All day I ate sweets and caught fish like there was no tomorrow. The skinny kid with the dark brown hair and darker eyes outfished everyone on the boat, much to my Uncle Holt's delight and amusement.

'Beginner's luck!' he'd shout, laughing loudly each time I caught one. The rod was speaking to me. It was alive with possibility. The kicking, bending life in my hands touched me then in the same way it does now.

There was one black spot on that perfect day and it troubled me. Each time a dogfish was brought to the boat, one of the men would lift a short club and whack the fish hard on the head. It was then unceremoniously dumped back into the sea.

'They're vermin,' I was told.

Instinctively I didn't like it. Even then, I could see no difference between that mini-shark and the other fish that were placed further up the fishing hierarchy. I liked their shape and colour and to me they fought just as hard as any other fish. Perhaps that's why when I'm lucky enough to catch one, it goes straight back into the water with a smile.

I'll never forget the biggest fish of that day. My lovely new rod was bent in an impossible arc as a large fish seized the bait. I heard for the first time the ritual stirrings among anglers when a large fish is on the line.

'Looks like a good 'un ... don't let it get off ... keep the rod high and the line tight ...' – all the obligatory advice handed out over generations and which I'm now guilty of chanting at my daughters.

After what seemed like ages, but was probably only five or ten minutes, of trying to crank the fish up from the bottom I wanted to give up: 'Uncle Holt, will you bring it up for me?'

'No, you must be a man. You must do it yourself,' came the firm reply. He smiled and coaxed me along. Bit by bit, inch by inch, I gained on the fish until we could see a flash of snow-white in the green depths.

The rod bucked and nodded under the pressure, but she held firm. So too did the little reel and line. I was so excited, everyone had stopped fishing and was peering over the side for a glimpse of the big fish being played by a wee boy.

Finally, with a supreme effort and with tired, sore arms, I pulled hard and the great fish thrashed the surface. It was gaffed and pulled aboard. It was a cod, over 10lbs in weight and very nearly the length of me. It seemed all head and cavernous mouth.

There was a buzz on the boat and great banter. The men shook my hand, slapped me on the back and praised my strength and courage. Uncle Holt led the way, telling them all they should be ashamed of themselves, outfished by a child.

I swelled with pride and must have been insufferable. Clearly I was the next big thing in fishing. This was only my first fishing expedition so it stood to reason that in a couple of weeks I'd be world class.

My brother met us at the slipway. He'd caught two fish which he said were rock cod. They weighed about 1lb each and were a really good catch off that harbour. He was proud of himself. He'd been denied the chance of going out in the boat and proved he could still catch fish.

His success went unnoticed. The talk was all about

me, of the talent and the funny childish things I'd said and of the big fish I'd caught. Stephen said nothing when he saw my cod. It was so big I couldn't lift it out of the boat.

THE ROD

Most middle-aged anglers have too many rods and not enough hair. It's sad but true and in both cases there is precious little we can do about it. But it's not our fault: fishing rods have lives of their own, strange, supernatural powers that lead us astray and loosen the tightest grip on any wallet.

Each has a voice, a Siren call all it's own. But unlike the horrible creatures of ancient mythology that sang so beautifully to lure sailors to their doom, you won't hear it at any conscious level. No, this is a subtle invasion of the mind, like mist softly rolling down a valley.

The craving for a new rod can strike at any time. The

fishing season may be months away, shining like a silver speck at the end of a long winter tunnel, yet there you are, full of the spirit of spring and the urge to accumulate yet more tackle.

Standing in the pale yellow light cast out from the tackle shop window, all thoughts of the tin of paint, or milk, or whatever you left home to buy are erased. The sleet falls on the dirty pavement and in you walk, pulled by the rod, like a fish on the line.

We've all done it. Wandered in for just a quick look, which lasts all afternoon. And like an alcoholic who can't pass the pub, we fool ourselves into believing we can stop at just one packet of hooks or a small box of weights.

Intoxicated, in a trance, the rod draws you on. You can only deny it for so long, toying with the floats, flies and spinners, but the sales assistant has your number. He can spot the wide eyes and smell the cash.

Sauntering past the rows of rods, it's impossible not to look. The Siren Song is irresistible. Arranged like a beauty pageant, they are displayed by height, make and exclusivity. They are perfumed with promise and cellulose.

Among the ranks one will catch your eye. A quiet little voice says 'pick me up', and then there's no putting it down. There's nothing you can do about it. The best advice is, try not to touch. Unfortunately, resistance is almost always futile and invariably costly.

Once the rod has you in *her* grasp – that soft, round, silky smooth cork handle will cast a spell. As you caress the glossy frame and gaze intently into her eyes, she'll whisper. And when you flex and bend her, making short, sharp casts in the cramped confines of the dimly lit shop, she'll seduce you with the call of another life. There you'll share the thrill of catching big fish and experience the joy of long, lazy summer days together. You're hooked.

The sales patter is all just words. It's nonsense: you've been hypnotised by a rod, by her slim, lithe form and dark good looks. She's sold herself. The credit card is produced, signed and accepted – the deal is done. You've just spent money you didn't have on a rod you didn't need.

Walking on air to the car, you haven't a care in the world. The rod is perched against the front passenger seat. She demands to sit there, to be seen. Smiling the smile of the smitten, you touch the rough cordura-covered tube that will keep her safe and sound for years to come: or until the lure of another leaves her cast aside in the garage.

It's freezing outside, but the rod is telling you it's June. You can hear her singing through the air, flicking a size 16 blue-winged olive at a wily old trout. He's rising with effortless regularity, nipping the insects off the surface just below a big willow tree. The rod sends the fly line into the air in snaking loops with a swish. It mingles with running water, dappled sunlight and birdsong. You're gone. The rod is singing your song.

Driving on automatic pilot, the daydream always begins to fade just as you reach home and start to figure out the best way to sneak her in past your wife. With very few exceptions, women don't get the rod thing. Shoes maybe, but a fishing rod for every conceivable situation is an alien concept. Spending hundreds of pounds on one can put a strain on relations – but it's more often the amount of time spent in her company, in pursuit of fishing dreams, that leads to divorce.

A lucky rod is an especially powerful thing. Everyone has one or had one. They are valuable far beyond the price paid for them. A rod and the memory of the fish it caught go hand in hand throughout the years.

Such a rod is often easy to spot. They usually fall in to the category of: 'They don't make 'em like that anymore.' A favourite rod has usually been in the hands of an angler and/or his family for a long time. It's invariably battered and faded. It's often heavy, a poker-stiff solid fibreglass relic in odd colours, like mustard or white. Often the threads hang loose from the eyes and the cork handle is pitted and blackened by the fishy hands of time. But to the owner, it's a thing of beauty, a friend forever.

I recently splashed out on a new fly rod to replace another expensive rod, which no longer suited my casting style. The old one was a beautiful American job but the action was too soft and floppy. So, after about ten years catching wild trout with her from the west of Ireland to the far north, I decided to let her go.

My first day out with the new one I caught no fish – even though we were only hunting stocked rainbows in a put-and-take fishery in Tyrone. That's another strange thing. The first fish is often the most difficult to catch on a new rod. Andy, my boat partner, took it for a cast. He smiled, slowly nodded his approval and quietly fished with it. He is a man of few words.

That left me flailing his long-time favourite fly rod. It was twice the weight and seemed ten times as stiff as mine.

'How do you fish with that brush shaft?' I said.

'I've caught a lot of trout on it,' came the terse reply.

I must have planted a seed though because, later that week, he went to the tackle shop and took a slightly longer version of my rod out on trial.

Strangely, it had no power over him. Andy said he was tempted but couldn't commit. Why should he change a rod that he was happy with? Maybe he's the exception that proves the rule. Some of us do it all the time.

I once had a very special rod. The funny thing is though that it wasn't even mine. It belonged to my big brother, but I loved it with a passion. I remember my first sight of it. Stephen rushed home one evening all excited with this prized rod in a thick cloth bag. He was sixteen, I was only ten.

It was unpeeled with a flourish in the bedroom we shared. I was instantly struck by the colour. It had a matt, dove-grey finish and looked silky smooth.

There were no eyes on it. 'It's a kit. I'm going to build it myself,' Stephen said with a satisfied grin. He was going to have a custom-built rod, a one-off. It was special already.

'You can help if you want,' he said, knowing that without the extra hands it would be impossible to make.

I was excited: this was a great treat. Stephen was brilliant at making Airfix aeroplanes. I would always make a mess with the glue but he never did. I knew he'd make a neat job and I was going to help him. I couldn't wait.

He slotted the two-piece blank together. It made a lovely soft, precise sound as it slid home. He flexed it vigorously for a few seconds.

'It's supposed to bend from tip to butt. That's for playing big fish,' he said. 'It's hollow fibreglass, just feel how light it is.'

This was my first touch. The cork handle, above and below the silver reel seat, was warm in my hands. It was as light as a feather and, it was whispering to me already. The writing on the base of the blank declared it to be a ten-foot salmon spinning rod made by Sundridge. I'm not certain but I seem to remember it also had a red map of Great Britain emblazoned on it.

There was absolutely no chance that it would ever be used for the purpose intended by the manufacturer. This rod would be employed exclusively for catching pike, the fish that we both rated above any other.

We propped the two blanks against a bed. Stephen reached for a crumpled paper bag and emptied its contents onto the bedspread. There, lay a tangled mess of chrome-coloured eyes that would be fitted onto 'our' rod. There was also a large wooden bobbin full of a yellow and black nylon thread. It complemented the dull grey rod perfectly. Finally, there was a small tin of clear cellulose varnish and a fine sable hair paintbrush to complete the kit.

It took quite a long time to make the rod. First the eye positions were measured out by Stephen and marked with a felt-tip pen. Then it was my turn to help. The first eye was laid on the blank. I held it in place with my thumb while my brother made a few turns of the thread to bind it to the rod.

'Now turn it slowly with me,' he said.

We rolled the rod. Stephen kept the thread tight, each turn firmly touching the next until the fine thread began to spread down the rod, giving the appearance of broad tape. It was then bound over a loop of thread. When we'd come far enough down the rod, the thread was cut and passed through that loop. It could then be pulled back under, between the whipping and the rod, to leave a seamless finish.

This labour of love was repeated upstairs every night after tea. There, surrounded by the lemon and white wood chip wallpaper and the beige curtains printed with brown birds of no particular kind, we worked together. It was quiet and intense. By the time the whipping process was finished, our four hands were perfectly co-ordinated.

The rod was binding us closer. We were at one with the vision and the job at hand. It was a rare and happy coincidence for two children separated by six years and a different take on life. We shared no friends and had little in common. I was often a burden because he was forced to take me with him on his outings. I would always be his junior, never able to compete on equal terms in football or anything else, except the one thing that united us: fishing. That was the one area where I could compete.

In the early years, our father used to take us pike

fishing. He was no sportsman. He used a boat rod for sea fishing and a huge fixed spool reel with nylon so thick it could easily have been used to string tennis rackets. When he was lucky enough to hook a fish it was winched to the bank without any fuss and little appreciation. The heel of his black rubber boots killed it with a brutal stamp. My father never got the spiritual side of fishing. For him it was all about eating the catch. For some that's enough.

I remember one evening when the three of us were fishing on the banks of the Newry Canal and Stephen caught a pike of about 4lbs. He'd run out of treble hooks and was using a long shank single and a bit of herring fillet.

This is the first time I remember being jealous. I was so envious I begrudged him the fish. 'How could he catch that fish on just one hook?' I wondered. And I stood there on the bank, surrounded by rushes and a light mist rising from the water.

I was fixed to the spot and staring – not for the last time – at my red and white plastic float. I was willing it to go under.

'He'd stand there all night if we let him,' said Stephen. My father and he laughed. They wanted to go but I uttered the Prayer of the Desperate for the first time that night.

'Just five more minutes, just one last cast,' I pleaded. There aren't enough minutes or casts in the world to satisfy an angler who can't catch a fish.

If we were separated by age Stephen and myself were also like chalk and cheese in other ways too. We even looked different. His hair was sandy brown, mine almost black. His eyes were a light grey-blue, but mine were polished coals. He used his brain – I used my fists. He was methodical, always able to move from A to B in his head without feeling the urge to skip straight to Z. It all made sense to him. There was a plan to follow, and in the case of the rod, he was good at it.

For me, then as now, nothing was clear and plans sort of evolved, took on a life of their own. Instinct and intuition are disastrous attributes when introduced to the world of do-it-yourself. I'd certainly have been left with bits over.

So we worked on, in the stillness of the bedroom. There was no radio, no TV to break the studied concentration. We were content to work together.

Applying the varnish to protect the thread was a tricky business. I turned the blank over and over while Stephen loaded the brush and touched the threads. By keeping it on the move it stopped drips forming. And as each was completed, the hairdryer quickly turned the liquid into a hard and glossy strip.

There was real pride when it was finished. Stephen squinted down the eyes of the assembled rod like they were the sights of a gun. They were perfectly in line and looked like they had been professionally fitted at the factory.

He stood up and brandished it like Excalibur – this was a mighty weapon: in the right hands a prodigious slayer of fish. He didn't know it, but I believed the right hands were my hands.

And my reward for the help and love I'd lavished on this enterprise?

'I'll let you have a cast with it when we go fishing on

Saturday, but on no account are you ever to take this rod out by yourself. If you break it I'll kill you. Do you understand?'

I said I did, but understood that it would be impossible for me not to take it. He didn't fish nearly so much as me and sure, wasn't it half mine anyway? I believed that morally I had a share, was entitled to it. He jealously guarded it in the same way we all love a new rod. But as the cork handle grows darker from use it can in time become just another fishing stick.

As the months rolled by I thought it had indeed become just that for Stephen. I regularly slipped it out of its corner in the garage. It silently insisted I take it. I knew he'd hammer me if I got caught, but that just added to the thrill of catching fish with it behind his back.

I was especially careful with it, except on the one occasion when I nearly lost it. There's a stretch of the River Bann which snakes alongside the golf course at Portadown. There's a deep corner fringed with lily pads on the far side and a little shingle beach opposite from which you can fish.

Like all my friends, I never used shop-bought rod rests. We'd always cut a Y-shaped branch and stick it into the bankside mud or prop the rod against a rock to keep the tip pointing at the sky. Finding a rod rest was part of the day's ritual. When the perfect stick was found, the bail arm on the reel would be left open to allow the fish to take line and Bob's your Uncle, you were fishing.

On the day in question I was with Brian Hobson, a

fishing pal and classmate. We shared a low boredom threshold and a strong sense of adventure. He'd caught a frog and I'd gone down the bank a short distance to see it. When I looked back I saw something moving in the river where I'd been fishing.

'That's my rod!' I roared as we both leaped to our feet and chased after it. The grey salmon spinning rod was sailing down the middle of the river. I'd forgotten to flick the bail arm over so when a pike took the dead bait there was nowhere else for the rod to go but into the river.

It was now well out of reach. Terrified of losing it and without thinking of the danger, I ran further downstream and waded in up to my middle. The water was shockingly cold. As the rod passed me, I reached out, grabbed it and struck. Happy days! The pike was still on the line and the rod was safe. Brian netted what we both had hoped was an enormous fish but which turned out to be a small one of about 6lbs.

It was a warm summer's day and I eventually dried out. It's funny how many days were warm and dry in childhood. Everything seems brighter looking back and the rod is there among the happy fragments of excited days filled with sunshine and innocence.

The rod is there with the pike, the fish that fired my imagination. In my boyhood mind, they lived in a mysterious, unseen realm. Down there, I could imagine them stalking their prey like big cats – the lily pads and pond weed provided cover just like the tall grass of the African plains. The roach, rudd, perch and bream were the antelope and wildebeest living in fear of ambush and sudden death.

It was that world of adventure and excitement I dreamed about when at school. On Saturdays the river drew me like a magnet. The bus ride to Portadown was an expedition and the long walk to Moneypenny's lock on the Newry Canal was an eternity for the boy who still lives in this head.

It's all too vivid. The thick scent of wet nettles and the sweet aroma of freshly cut grass quickly replaced the smell of traffic fumes. As we walked away from the bridge in the town, the tower of St Mark's church grew smaller and the sound of laughter and fish-talk grew stronger.

Beyond the boat club, we'd always stop at the cement steps to catch bait. This was a small platform where a big drainage ditch overflowed into the river. The pipes spewed dirty water into the river under our feet and there were always the footprints of rats in the mud. We'd take pot shots at them with our catapults when we got the chance. We didn't care that it was and still is an ugly little blot on the landscape. For us it was a good place to catch bait quickly and move on.

There was a brief period around May when we never had to worry about the availability of bait. About that time, spawning roach shoaled in unimaginable numbers. They were so dense that in places we could scoop them directly out of the river with a landing net.

Below Knock Bridge on the Bann, just across the fields from Moneypenny's lock, there's a set of rapids that tails off into deep water. We used to stand in the middle of that run and watch as their navy-blue backs surged past us in waves. There were so many that they were bouncing off our wellie boots as they made their way upstream. On the bend, where the water was fastest, the old, unfit and dying were forced onto their sides and jammed against the rocky bank.

On those days we'd spend too much time there. It was an idyllic place. The sight and sound of the running water was always a strong draw.

But that was the exception. Our journey almost always took us to the Point of Whitecoat. This is where the River Cusher, Newry Canal and the River Bann meet. The pace always quickened as we approached it. We'd march on accompanied by the larks singing high in a wide blue sky.

I still love spying them out, little black specks in the heavens. Hand over eyes in salute, you wait for them to fold their wings and drop like a stone to within a few feet of the field. The wings open like a parachute and the little daredevil sails back to its tiny nest in a meadow spangled with buttercups and daisies.

It was always a hard choice where to fish. Mostly we found holes in the duckweed and lilies along the Cusher. Sometimes we'd walk all the way along it, cross the bridge below Moneypenny's and then trudge all the way back towards the town.

At Moneypenny's the ancient lock gates were long gone but the stone chamber and the derelict lock-keeper's cottage survived. It sits just yards from the main rail link between Belfast and Dublin. It was the age of steam and fast trains that killed the canals in the nineteenth century.

In my childhood, more than a hundred years later, all trace of the towpath had long since disappeared under a tangle of bracken, nettles and trees. For us it was a jungle and it made the walk up the peninsula between the Cusher and the canal a slow and sweaty expedition.

But the reward was worth it. We could fish in both the river and the canal because they were just yards apart. That was the best fishing option but the worst for the feet. It added miles to the journey because at that time there was no bridge at the Point of Whitecoat to carry you back to the Portadown bank – to get home you had to retrace your steps, a journey of several miles.

This then was my hunting ground with the rod and my friends. We were keen but clueless. We rarely caught anything over 4lbs and when we did, it was always beaten about the head and laid on the bank – a potent symbol of pre-pubescent bravado. We were the Great White Hunters: the pike were olive-and-cream trophies, carried home to impress Mum.

On the odd occasion we did encounter a big fish – anything over 10lbs was massive – it was usually a disaster. Fish were lost at the net or because we'd forgotten the net; lost through overexcitement and inexperience; because the tackle was cheap and/or broken or countless other stupid reasons.

The ones that got away are always remembered better than those landed, especially when they disappeared at a rate of knots into the weeds in a huge swirl.

All fishermen, regardless of age believe, in the big one, whether it's there or not. It's the spark in the imagination that drives us on. When you're ten, the big one is GIGANTIC.

I saw it myself. A huge pike had taken my bait and was swimming away with it close to the surface. I could see her heading directly towards a waterhen in open water. I was certain the pike was for attacking the bird. I ran down the bank, picked up the rod and struck. There was a sickening crack as the line snapped and an explosion on the surface, like a hand grenade had been thrown into the river. It was a monster.

The biggest fish I ever hooked in my childhood was played on the rod. The river was the colour of milky coffee, stirred up by an autumn flood. I was fishing close to the mouth of the Cusher and saw the rod tip twitch sharply round. I gave it a little line, then tightened up and struck.

Suddenly the fish charged off down river with the flow. It was so powerful and fast I was forced to walk after it. The rod was bent hard.

My friends were all round me, shouting and looking for a first sight of it.

It was then we remembered there was no landing net. I'd forgotten it. The pike began to thrash about on the surface near a bend in the steep bank. It was close to, if not over 20lbs. None of us had seen a fish anywhere near that big before. The head was huge, the excitement and suspense, unbearable. How was I going to get it out?

We noticed a small lip, or shelf, of sand at the bottom of the bank. 'I'll try to beach her here,' I said. There was a fierce flow running, but by sheer luck, the huge fish came alongside it and actually beached herself.

What to do next? The fish was half in, half out of the water. The bank was too steep and slippery to walk down. There was a raging torrent running so if anyone fell in, they'd be a goner. I handed my rod, The Rod, to Brian and decided to try to get to the fish.

As I began to climb down, the great fish could see me and began to lift her enormous head and tail in an arc. She was trying to get off the sand. Two or three more times she did the same and little by little her heavy, beautifully camouflaged body began to turn.

I was halfway to her, my wellie boots slipping and sliding on the muddy bank, when it happened. She made a violent lunge. Brian was holding the line so tight that the nylon snapped like cotton.

It felt like I was watching it in slow motion. With all resistance gone, she was able to turn her big, bony head and roll off the sand. Her massive frame was weightless again in the dirty water. She was gone.

I cried. The tears of disappointment, anger and frustration were unstoppable. I didn't blame my friend; it was just my rotten luck. If only I'd remembered the landing net we might have landed her.

The pain of losing a big fish is gut-wrenching no matter what your age. There is a replay mechanism in the brain designed specially for such occasions. Over and over it will show you the parting vision of your prize catch. Again and again it will be accompanied by heartache. It's a nightmare.

I remember that fish better than any other I ever actually landed on the rod. Over the years I had a secret partnership with it. It was always left back in its place after our weekend adventures. I lost it when my brother moved away from home and took it with him. It was packed off with the rest of his belongings. A lovely metallic blue, nine footer made by ABU took its place. But it wasn't the same.

The memory of the rod faded with time and soon it was out of sight, out of mind. It was to tell me a different tale many years later when I saw it for the last time. By then Stephen was a golf-playing family man, whose only interest in fishing was satisfied by a once-a-year outing with me.

It was Saturday and I'd called into his house in Banbridge with a brace of woodcock, and a pheasant that Andy and I had shot in the wilds of south Armagh.

I was setting the birds down on the windowsill outside the kitchen when for some reason I turned my head and it caught my eye, or perhaps it whispered. I saw the discarded butt of the rod first. There was an instant flash of recognition at seeing my old friend.

The years had not been kind. It was covered in cobwebs and dust and jammed into a crevice below the flat roof of the carport.

The matt-grey blank was caked in grime.

Worse still – I saw that it was broken. There was a

ragged fracture in the middle of the bottom section.

I stood for quite a time just taking it in: looking at what I didn't want to see.

Then the questions: How did it happen and when? Did he contact the Sundridge factory to see if they had a replacement section? Why didn't he tell me about it? There was also an odd mixture of disappointment and sadness. So much of my childhood was mixed up with it, so many happy memories. It was a break with the past.

Stephen had no idea how much I loved that rod. I never told him about the big fish I'd lost with it or the small ones caught with it. I never even told him I'd seen it broken. And I never told him how much I valued it, because as a wee boy, I'd built it with my big brother.

Then again, maybe he did know. Maybe the rod had spoken to him too. And just maybe, he'd kept its shattered remains as a memento: a reminder of a time when we were bound together as tightly as the yellow and black threads on the rod itself.

WHERE'S THE
CATCH?

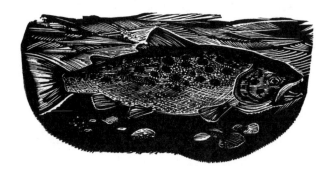

Walking along the shoreline, I could see a small group of big trout cruising in the shallows. They were sipping down midge pupae in the flat calm. Only the slightest ripple betrayed their presence almost within touching distance: that and the oily disturbance created by a big tail beating away from below. Instinctively, I stopped and crouched.

The biting March wind was crazing the water, leaving a trace like wire netting just a few feet beyond the hungry fish. Sheltering in the lee of the slope and with the added protection of a thick blackthorn hedge, I could feel the early spring sun, carrying with it the promise of summer heat.

I stayed hunkered down and resisted the temptation to begin casting. It took resolve, I was itching to begin but they'd be easily spooked in such clear water and there was nowhere for me to hide. So I waited for a couple of minutes, watching through polarising sunglasses as they deftly picked the hatching buzzers off the top.

These over-wintered trout were by no means the stupid pellet-fed fish that had originally been stocked into the lake from the hatchery. They might have been that a year or two earlier, but liberty, a natural diet and exposure to fly fishermen had returned them to the wild.

To be successful, I'd have to put a bit of distance between them and me, then I could lay a trap. I quickly retraced my footsteps in an arc, past the daffodils nodding in the breeze at the top of the bank and up past some scruffy sheep. Now on the hill, I was directly above the fish and able to use the hedge for cover.

Seeing big fish close enough to cover with a fly is one of the great fishing joys. It makes the fingers tremble. Because it doesn't happen that often, it can mess with your head. You can get overeager, overexcited. The arm that lands a dry fly with effortless ease and with pinpoint precision to an 'ordinary' trout can just as easily overshoot or slap the line onto the water like a novice when there's a big fish within range.

Having one chance, to do it right first time, under pressure, is the fishing equivalent of a three-foot putt to win the Open Championship – memorable when it goes in; unforgettable when it doesn't.

Bigger than average fish always make me especially nervous. These trout looked about 4-5lbs and my hands were shaking as I cut off my team of three flies. One fly and one good cast, I thought. I tied on a size 16 emerger. Shaw's Lake in County Armagh is home ground and I knew the dark olive pattern would probably work.

Then, sitting comfortably on the grassy knoll, insulated from the cold and damp by neoprene chest waders, I began to cast. I wanted to land the fly line on the field and drop only the 4lb tippet on the water, laying an unusual ambush to intercept the trout. This way they wouldn't see the fly line as it came down. Nor could they feel or hear it hitting the water.

I made the cast, the line curled neatly and turned over the long leader. The emerger landed like thistledown. Perfect: but would they take the bait?

They were all around it, taking insects to the left, to the right, in front and behind but ignoring my artificial fly. In the still water they had too much time to inspect it and, as looked likely, to reject it.

Some say trout are smart, I prefer to think of them as acutely aware of what looks right. They have an instinct for survival. We know it's highly developed, but even then they can surprise you – on one memorable occasion I was stalking a rainbow trout in similar conditions: flat calm and bright. He was mopping up daddy-long-legs blown onto the lake from the neighbouring fields.

Everything looked right to me: the leader was well degreased and was under the water, the fly was half drowned in the membrane where water meets air. As he approached I tweaked the line and sent out a tiny pulse. He head-and-tailed over the real thing a couple of feet away and then came up right underneath my fly. To my astonishment the fish lifted the artificial on the neb of his nose then dropped back under, leaving it still floating.

He'd just given me a two-fish-fingered salute – and it looked like it was happening again. My little emerger was being ignored and soon began to sit lower and lower in the water. Then, just as it broke the surface tension and began to sink, a trout seized it. The line went hard and the water churned white as I lifted into him.

The movement must have made his mind up for him. The natural pupae rise and fall in the water column all their lives. By sheer fluke I'd managed to achieve the effect at the exact moment a fish was passing. It looked right so he snapped it up.

He led me a merry dance for a few minutes until I had him lying on his side on the water's edge - an excellent brown trout easily twenty inches long. In the sunlight, his gill covers flashed iridescent green. The back was olive-brown and the firm belly, a warm buttery gold.

As I looked at him and basked in the thrill of having caught him, I knew I couldn't kill him. Suddenly it was as clear as the bible-black spots on his back. I didn't have to kill him just because he was a big fish. In fact, it was for that very reason that I had to put him back.

I turned out the tiny hook from the corner of his mouth and cradled the weightless body in my hands until his strength returned. As I let him go, and watched his dark shape disappear into memory, it felt good.

Unusually, that day I also didn't feel the need to keep fishing. The one fish, well caught, was enough. (Or was it that the commotion had forced the big fish out of reach?) Anyway, later, as I wore the contented grin of the seriously self-satisfied, I fancied I'd cracked another rung on the evolutionary fishing ladder.

It's said that when you start fishing, all you want to do is catch a fish – any fish. After that, you want to catch a lot of fish, regardless of size. When that's no longer enough, you must have a big fish. But the ultimate prize, when you are at the top of the sport, is to catch the impossible fish.

He's always that pig of a trout hidden from cast by an overhanging branch or always just upwind and out of range on a lough. It's funny, but the things you most want are all too often just beyond reach. The disappointments, setbacks and near misses are all steps on the road to success. They make the special moments even sweeter when they do come.

My victory was more improbable than impossible but it was an important fish nonetheless, because ever since, I've never had any difficulty releasing fish. And the funny thing is the more I do it, the easier it gets.

Such moments are among the best reasons I can think of for fishing. They are part and parcel of the constant stream of small surprises and discoveries that makes the pursuit so unpredictable. Those brief insights, where the veil is lifted and you get a peek at things that have been hidden, are a mind opener.

Epiphany is like staring at one of those patterned pictures where you are supposed to see something else. You cannot imagine what it is until you really see it, recognise the face of Christ or the bald man smiling out from a sea of coffee beans.

There are rare snapshots in time, when dawn breaks on the solitude of a still lough, when the wind breathes through the trees or the swallows twitter overhead and when it is possible to look out, look up and see the face of God.

His image is there in the unique pattern of a wild trout, the porcelain belly of a pike and the silver flanks of the humble roach. It is impossible not to be moved by the spirit of the fish and their home.

I read somewhere about the hunting tradition among native Americans where they ask the spirit of their dead quarry for forgiveness and even now, when I kill a fish, I often find myself doing it as quickly as possible and saying 'sorry' out loud. It doesn't help the fish, but oddly, it does help me.

I had the great fortune to talk to a real-life American Indian recently. Don Tenoso is a descendant of Sitting Bull, the Indian chief against whom General Custer made his Last Stand. Don's people, the Lakota Sioux, have a similar take on life.

'We see no difference between a fish, or a buffalo,' said Don, an artist who'd come to the Ulster American Folk Museum in Omagh with an exhibition of Native American artefacts.

'We say thanks to the creature for feeding our families,' he said, dressed in black and sporting the traditional braids in his long black hair.

Don is a fisherman too and it wasn't long before we were talking about pike, trout and the other species we had in common. His dark brown eyes sparkled as he talked of the ponds on the reservation where bass had been stocked and abandoned and where now huge fish were to be caught.

But he also spoke of the connection between the Indian people and the land. The fact that in his culture, the rock has a spirit – it symbolises stamina and permanence.

It's a connection most of us have lost. But seeing a deer, a rabbit, a trout or even us as small parts of the wider world is a big thought. In fishing, and in life, giving something back is its own reward.

It is important to make the distinction between wild and stocked fish.

A wild fish carries with it the cachet of 24 carat gold. Such fish are the hallmark of quality, the Picasso signature on a work of art. Stocked fish are introduced to lakes by man and the fact that they are reared by us, not Mother Nature, affects their value – at least in the mind of the angler.

If a farm-reared brown or rainbow trout is caught, killed and eaten it can easily be replaced, restocked. The wild fish are irreplaceable so at the very least we should think for a moment about whether it's really necessary to take them home.

Not everyone gets the idea of catch and release for wild

trout, where the fish survive on an ecological knife-edge. Some can't see beyond the dinner plate.

Don told me that when the Europeans were colonising the Wild West, his people called them 'fat stealers' because they always took more than they needed and what wasn't theirs in the first place.

Little has changed, for some at least. On the big Irish loughs, such as Mask or Melvin, there is no bag limit for these genetically pure trout. You can keep as many fish as greed allows. There is plenty of scope for gluttony. These pristine jewels in the crown of Irish fishing are replete with leopard-spotted predators whose ancestors arrived with the melting snow of the last Ice Age.

Long before man set foot on this island, these wild and desolate places have been their home. Stone Age man speared and trapped them to survive and modern man, armed with a fly rod fashioned from space age graphite, is still chasing them.

We are motivated by the same primal need to hunt and gather but we don't need to kill to survive. We go out into the waves to meet nature head-on and live to tell the tale. For some it is enough just to be afloat in that separate world: for all of us the need to do it runs deep.

But for a few, it is also a place to take without thought, to fish without thinking of tomorrow and to kill for the sake of it. As well as no bag limit, there is no fee to be paid for the privilege of exploring some of the finest trout water in the world. Therein lies a problem.

Just watch the queue in an 'eat-all-you-can-for-a-fixed-price' restaurant and you'll get the picture. Plates piled higher with more food than anyone can eat. Human nature being what it is, the eyes will always be bigger than the belly. Lay on a banquet of trout fishing and you're certain some of the guests will shame you.

It's particularly bad during what's known as 'duffer's fortnight'. Wild brown trout are rightly regarded as a difficult species to catch with an artificial fly but for that short period in May and June, they seem to lose that highly developed sense of survival. They become fixated by the mayfly and can be caught with relative ease – on some days at least.

It's the same too for the Sonaghan – the unique, exquisite trout that swim the deep waters of Lough Melvin. Cupped between the borders of Counties Leitrim and Fermanagh, the lough is full to bursting with these incredible creatures.

For most of the year they are far below the reach of any artificial fly. Huge shoals of these sombre-coloured trout feed like herring, straining the rich plankton blooms from the open lough. In summer, these black-finned, soot-smudged brownies rise from the darkness into the upper layers and attack flies with such savage aggression that you'd think they'd been starved for months.

They average only ten inches but fight with the power of trout twice their size. Sonaghan are for my money the fastest taking trout on the planet, even the sharpest angler won't hook all they attract. They can hit the flies so hard the rod will jolt almost out of your hand and yet they'll avoid being hooked. One in three is a good average – for me at least.

By midsummer, the sport can be frantic. There are sometimes so many within reach of the fly fisher that they can be caught two and three at a time, like mackerel on feathers.

For a very short time they are vulnerable to even the most ordinary of anglers. Unlike primitive man, who knew when to stop, when enough was enough, there are a few 'civilised' anglers who don't, and that's a pity.

There is nothing wrong with killing trout to eat yourself or to give to family or friends. In fact, it is a right and proper thing that fish should be taken and eaten. It completes the circle. But it is wrong to kill more than you will eat. That's just a simple law of nature.

There is plenty of greed too in the world of salmon fishing. Fly anglers like to blame everyone else for the demise of the wild Atlantic salmon. Trawling at sea, netting in estuaries and poaching in the rivers are decried loudly.

Some say that catch and release doesn't work, that the salmon will die anyway. They say the cost of the fishing is such that keeping the black and chrome prize is a fisherman's reward, his right. And sure, the argument goes, there are so few fish taken on the fly or spinner that our impact on stocks is minimal – wrong.

The research proves that when handled properly, or to put it accurately, not handled at all, salmon will survive being hooked and played. Indeed one tagged fish in Scotland was caught THREE times on its way to spawn.

We are only fooling ourselves when we claim to make

no impact on stocks. The figures from the Salmon Research Station at Bushmills in County Antrim suggest that as much as fifty percent of the spring run on some rivers may be taken by anglers. That's half the total number of a dwindling stock taken on rod and line.

It's up to the individual to decide if he wants to take fish for the table and it's right that he should have that privilege. But if everyone thought about the good they might do by returning just one fish it just might make a difference. It isn't about what we inherit – it's about what we leave.

There will always be a few bad apples that'll take more than they should but they mustn't be allowed to spoil the barrel. Most of us are united by an abiding passion for the fish. We care deeply about the quality of the water they live in and have a strong affinity with the wild places that provide them with a home and us with an escape route.

We all live for the few, all too short hours, every weekend when we can shed the sophistication of twenty-first century living and come face to face with the world of our ancestors.

It's a primitive rite of passage and, like the followers of all religions, we have faith. We are eternal optimists because without the hope of success, the slightest chance of encountering ephemeral creatures in an unknown element, we wouldn't even pull on our wellies.

We'll talk for hours on a bankside to fellow disciples that we've never met before and probably never will again, just because we share a passion for angling.

The best of them turn the mobile phone off, or better still, leave it in the car. They haven't stopped the motor at the first available hole in the hedge and fished with rods propped against the boot while the stereo pollutes the silence.

It's the Tesco approach: on tap, on your doorstep, convenience fishing. You can keep that!

No, the best fishing, whether it is with a maggot for roach, bream or perch or with an artificial fly for salmon, trout or even pike, is to be found in the wild places. On a lake, beyond the sound of traffic; in the shade of an ancient chestnut tree on a lonely river; or huddled on a silent, frostbitten shore in February, the place adds value and meaning.

That isn't to say that the setting is everything. I can never really trust anyone who says: 'I don't have to catch a fish. It's enough just to be out there in beautiful surroundings.' I fancy it's a circumstance with which they have to contend all too often and of necessity they have grown philosophical about the absence of prey.

Somebody said that a great day must have a fish in it somewhere. He spoke for me too. To catch a fish is proof of life and a confirmation of faith. And sometimes if you are truly blessed, you learn that just one fish, well caught, is enough.

OFF THE MAP

DAY ONE

The digital clock on the dashboard read 4.29am. In four and a half hours' time I'd be on the shores of Lough Corrib. Beyond the long dark road lay four days of fabulous fly fishing, the friendship of fellow anglers and the nearest I'm ever likely to get to freedom.

Driving away from the house, I sipped at hot coffee from behind the wheel. My only company was a low set tangerine moon and the eye-watering fumes from the two-stroke oil and petrol I'd spilled on the carpet. It didn't matter. The big lake in the far west of Ireland was drawing me to her like a mother with open arms.

Speeding through the night, Billy Joel appeared on the stereo and caught the mood: 'These are the days to hold onto, but we won't although we'll want to ...' Amen.

I felt a delicious thrill of anticipation. Through the barren winter months, I had been aching for this trip and now, finally, I was on the brink of adventure. All through that close season the wild brown trout of Lough Corrib had been eking out a living, devouring shrimp, water louse and snails among the limestone rocks in the cold depths.

Now, in late March, with the duckfly pupae rising to the surface to hatch, the trout were following them up and feeding on the tiny morsels by the million. When there's a good hatch, when the days are warm and the winds light, the adult buzzers hang like palls of smoke over the naked, early spring trees.

Up close, these insects can be heard as a low buzz in the still air – hence the name. And over the rich silt beds, or duckfly holes, where the adults lay their eggs, countless wriggling pupae continue to ascend the water column.

Their mass migration and transformation into large black midges attracts big numbers of trout into their small hatching areas. It's a recipe for great fishing. It's all a question of time and place.

The phone call from my friend Ronnie Patterson the night before had confirmed the prospects were good. I was on my way to join him and a band of top-notch fishermen from Scotland and Wales.

Conditions weren't ideal. The weather was a little cold, the wind a bit too strong and the hatches a shade patchy, but even so, the lads had been catching wild brown trout on epoxy buzzers – a beautifully technical method of copying the look and movement of the duckfly pupae.

My head was buzzing with that news and from the petrol fumes on the way into Sligo as dawn approached. In the shadow of the hills above Glencar Lake and opposite the grey plateau of Ben Bulben, a hot orange sun rose in an ice-blue sky. It was the only highlight on the road to Oughterard – the dreary towns in-between are only markers on the journey west.

Past Galway city, at Moycullen, the mobile phone rang: 'Where are you?' It was Ronnie's unmistakable Lurgan brogue and minimalist approach to conversation on the mobile. We were to spend the day in a boat together and he wanted to make sure I wasn't going to cost him time by making him wait at the jetty.

At a pound a minute for the international call, he sounded like a telegram: 'Great, five minutes away. See you at breakfast.' He was gone.

The car park was littered with friends and the paraphernalia of fishing when I reached Lakeview Country House on the Corrib shore just outside Oughterard. Among the ritual handshakes, smiles and warm greetings from men I'd not seen since the same time last year, it felt like a conference, every bit as idiosyncratic as a Star Trek convention.

We weren't planning 'to boldly go where no man has gone before', but we were hoping to find the sort of uncharted fishing experience that's out of this world.

Over the inevitable copious and carnivorous Full Irish, the chatter was all about the weather and the fish. The dining room had an air of excitement, laughter and expectation that only the prospect of a day in paradise can bring.

Among the clatter of knives and forks and the rasp of buttering toast, plans were being hatched for the day ahead. George Barron is always at the heart of such discussions. A Scot by birth, he lives in and fishes for Wales and is among the finest tiers of flies anywhere in the British Isles.

He has that rare capacity possessed only by the elite: he can read the mind of trout, or at least he can make up their mind for them by forcing them to take his fly.

The group knows this and looks to him. I watched him articulate the finer points of a figure of eight retrieve, illustrated with the delicate finger movements of a harpist. Eyebrows stretched upwards into his bald and rapidly tanning forehead, his serious eyes twinkling on fire. He was at breakfast, but his mind was in another place altogether.

Most at the table have been crossing the Irish Sea on the annual duckfly pilgrimage for nearly twenty years. Beside me sat the droll, affable and irrepressible Dai Willie, one of that hard core who never miss this event. He's a great, barrel-chested, middle-aged man with a cunning ability to catch trout. When he fished for Wales, the English called him 'Di-saster', because he was unbeatable on his day.

The same can be said for Scotsman Stan Headley, a writer by profession and a famous inventor of trout flies. His patterns, like the Doubry and the Melvin Octopus, are to be found in thousands of flyboxes across the UK and Ireland. But quite apart from that, he's great craic to share a boat with – as I was to find out later.

The morning was grey with a chill north-easterly when Ronnie and I left the jetty. He struck his familiar pose, standing in the stern with a hand on the tiller, the other in a pocket and his dark, intense eyes fixed on the horizon.

We had a plan and headed straight for a duckfly hole twenty minutes away from the pier at Lal Faherty's Angling Centre. The 15-horse Mariner hummed as the 19-foot *Angler's Fancy* skipped over the light waves of Portacarron Bay.

Ronnie headed for the eastern shore, past Inishcash and then round Ard Point. We hung a right at Rabbit, went past Goat and Kid and with Flynn Island at our back, we entered the mouth of the canal. In the lee of the shoreline we picked a course into a hot spot which, according to Ronnie, had been 'bubbling with trout' the previous evening.

Duckfly were indeed hatching. The wings rust red for maybe three seconds when they hit the air but dissolving to greyish white as if by magic before buzzing off. A single housemartin, the first of the year, swooped overhead as it too fed on the little insects.

The water was flat calm and the only sound was the serenade of birdsong. At last, we were fishing; the great escape had begun.

After a couple of drifts and no signs of fish we headed back to investigate the light and dark waters of the limestone reefs around Flynn, a noted duckfly area. Not today.

Fishing is a bit like buying a house – there are three crucial requirements – location, location, location. The map of Lough Corrib reveals only the contours of shoreline and the tapestry of 365 Islands that pepper her 44,000-acre surface. But the place we were looking for can't be read off a page. It's physical but hidden. You have to know where the duckfly holes are, when the hatches happen and even then you need a bit of luck. It's also about reading the lake and looking for clues.

Gulls will often lead you to fish because when they are eating flies from the surface, the trout are usually doing the same. But in the absence of visual evidence, like birds, flies or rising fish, it's a case of playing your best guess.

'Where do you want to go?' said Ronnie with characteristic directness. 'Let's try the back of Inchiquin,' I suggested.

My hunch took us north, into Greenfields Bay, under the causeway and out the back of Inchiquin Island, where we could pull wet flies over the shoals – and it worked.

The action was unbelievably fast and furious all day long. With no flies hatching, the trout were eager to accept the Claret Dabblers, Bibios and Connemara Blacks we offered them. The time passed as if in a dream. Hands and arms worked with the sort of integration experienced by long distance runners – the motion committed to muscle memory.

On a huge lake, under a big sky and in a landscape that stretched to the Maamturk Mountains on the western horizon, time slowed and the world condensed into the few short feet at the end of our fly lines.

Drift after drift, fish after lemon-bellied, heavily spotted fish, we journeyed, zigzagging our way down the breeze, and along the southern shore of Tanai Island.

Close in, where blackened limestone boulders poked from the lake like rotten teeth, the trout were lying in the dark water. They'd send the waves into turmoil, as their deeply forked tails pushed towards the pulsing flies.

When they took the fly and ripped line from the fingertips in a savage race for rocky cover, the blood stirred and the breath quickened. It was exhilarating.

Ronnie's not the sort to wax lyrical about the spiritual nature of where we were or what we were doing, but over lunch, sitting on a long, flat limestone pavement at the water's edge, he looked into the distance.

Glancing down occasionally, he shelled a hard-boiled egg from the picnic basket with his rough hands, hardened by years of laying bricks: 'This is the life,' he said. 'The rest is all just marking time.'

We were now both in another place, off the map. The afternoon flew by with the speed that only happens all too rarely. By seven o'clock in the evening, I couldn't lift my arm for another cast – fifteen hours on the road and constant casting on an unsteady lough had finally beaten me, but Ronnie wasn't finished yet.

As we approached Lees Point, he swung the bow in towards the shore and pointed it at a half-submerged barbed wire fence. 'This is always a good place for a trout,' he said.

The Claret Dabbler barely hit the water when a lovely fish of about 1½lbs hit it. I cheered and he laughed.

Perfect.

DAY TWO

Waking to the sound of birdsong on a day when your only care will be where to fish on a wild Irish lough is like winning the lottery. Pulling the curtains aside for the first peep at the weather and seeing a high cover of candyfloss clouds floating on a gentle breeze is nature's great panacea.

My back was stiff as I stretched out under the duvet, but the baggage of life that's usually bolted to my shoulders was gone. There'd be plenty of time for it to be collected and reattached with every mile on the way back to the world, but for now it was forgotten and irrelevant.

When you chase trout, there is no need of a career, mortgage, car or any of the other distractions that clog life and stifle the spirit. All you need is a rod in your hand and hope in your heart.

There is tremendous simplicity and joy in understanding that you can kick the stuff that shortens life. An ancient Babylonian proverb claims: 'The Gods do not deduct from man's allotted span, the hours spent in fishing.' That's a fine justification for this noble sport as an investment in your own future.

If it's true, my boat partner for the day is a good candidate for immortality. Like all obsessive anglers, Alan Hill spends a great deal of time on the water. He's an ace angler who fished for Scotland in international competitions. Alan is a giant of a man, a big, burly policeman over six feet tall but he ties flies with the skill and finesse of a micro-surgeon.

Little wonder then, that I was a shade over-awed and nervous about fishing with him. I needn't have worried.

'Do you have any epoxy buzzers?' he enquired. I opened my fly box and he scanned the ones I'd tied badly and the others I'd bought.

'Take some of these,' he said and generously offered me several of his own beautifully crafted pupae.

'They'll work,' he said confidently as we walked to the boat.

There are some people you meet and instantly take to – I had just met one.

Leaving the jetty, Alan clapped his hands together, rubbed them together vigorously and said: 'I love days like this, heading out to places that you've never been before, it's great.'

The Corrib was working her magic. We smiled and took in our surroundings. The rusty pins that mark the rocky shallows all over the lough glided by. Far to the north, past Inchagoill, Inishannagh and Inishmicatreer, Ashford Castle was invisible in the early spring mist.

Way out west, the mountains of Connemara were just thin silvery lines in the gloom. Heading east, we were thinking of the sheltered waters at the back of Inchiquin and hoping to pull vivid colour from another world.

I drove us flat out, directly to Greenfields Bay and out to Tanai Island where Ronnie and I had had all the action. Just when you think you've cracked it, fishing has a way of knocking you back. I couldn't get the trout interested in the wet flies that they were so keen on just twenty four hours earlier.

Alan, on the other hand, was calling them up from the depths with startling regularity. On every drift, he'd have technicoloured trout swirling and splashing.

I watched but couldn't match him. He constantly changed flies between drifts, altering patterns, profile and shape. It's the sort of approach born from competition angling, where tactics, lines and flies are methodically and repeatedly changed until the fish are found.

I've been fortunate over the years to meet and fish with some of the best anglers in the British Isles. They are all incredibly perceptive and intuitive about the nature of the fish they pursue. Alan was one more to add to the list.

We were fishing with similar flies in the same water and yet the trout were drawn to him. It was no mystery though. Put any talented amateur on a football pitch with the likes of Beckham, Ronaldo and Co and the difference will be plain enough.

When you are lucky enough to be in such company it's best to watch and listen. The experience is worth more when you learn from it.

Well into the afternoon, the wind eased, the air warmed a fraction and the buzzers began to hatch. We switched tactics and put on the little pupae patterns that Alan had tied in his home in Ayrshire.

In a small duckfly hole between Kid and Flynn Islands we found fish – or rather, Alan did. With only a pin ripple on the surface, the boat was almost static. He allowed the flies to fall slowly through the water where they were picked off by the feeding trout. The takes were terrifying. There's no need to strike. The trout hook themselves and in a nanosecond the supple line is transformed into a hard wire cutting the water at speed.

I couldn't get it to work until Alan tactfully offered some advice.

'I was out with George *(Barron)* yesterday and he showed me how to fish these buzzers,' he said.

'What you do is cast, like so,' and he sent the flies snaking out.

'Now you let them fall and just keep in touch with a slow figure of eight retrieve.'

I sat my rod down and watched the master class.

'The trout want them falling like the natural pupae, so when they've dropped as far as the line will let them you give several short quick pulls of the fly line,' he continued and tugged it about five times with his left hand.

'That draws the pupae back up in the water so they can fall again. That way you get them to fall more than once every cast and it increases your chances,' he said.

Eureka! It was as if a light had just been switched on. I now had a clear picture of what was happening below the ripple. When you can see the fly in your imagination, understand how it should look and make that happen, it tips the balance in the fisherman's favour.

Success was almost immediate. On just one drift in a little duckfly hole less than half the area of a football pitch we caught five glorious trout.

The savagery of the take – the point where the fly and the fly fisherman are inserted into the trout and the mysterious world they inhabit, was heart-stopping.

Only sex, drugs and fishing have such power to make you catch your breath, let go the conscious self and disappear into rapture.

Afterwards, in the comfort of an armchair, after a hot meal and in front of a turf fire, Alan, the other addicts and me talked endlessly about the fish and the shared experience. When you aren't fishing, the next best thing to it is talking about it. And there was plenty of that.

DAY THREE

I opened my eyes again to the sound of birdsong and a strong feeling that the year, too, was wakening up. There was a strong sense that a big wheel was turning.

On the islands and in the bays, the sights and sounds of spring were everywhere. The Blackthorn, the Mother of the Wood, wore the first faint dusting of blossom. In a week or so it would be as thick as snow on her branches, but for now it looked like icing sugar lightly sprinkled through a sieve.

The Lady of the Wood, the silver birch, carried with her the delicate blush of green buds on flimsy burgundy-tinged branches. Her white trunks caught the light among the drab ash, beech and oaks. They still clung to the dead leaves and seed cases, left parched and brittle from the previous autumn.

The wheel was turning slowly in real time; the sort laid down over millennia by the seasons. It doesn't bear any relation to the minutes and seconds of our daily working lives. We try to squeeze the juice from the day, wringing the clock like a wet cloth and yet there is never enough of it to go around. We drive faster cars, buy time-saving appliances, shift loads more work in less and less time and still we come up short.

We are time poor and all the poorer for it. Out on this timeless landscape nothing is rushed. Each bird, insect and plant has it's own time and place. Three days into the trip I too was on Corrib Time. Without a watch, I'd eat when I was hungry and return to the B&B when I was tired.

A pair of Canada Geese honked noisily on a stiff-winged flypast at Devenish Island. 'The mountains look beautifully clear this morning,' I shouted over the roar of my engine to Stan Headley, puffing away on his pipe at the bow.

'That's not necessarily a good thing,' he mused in a deep Scottish brogue. 'It means the air's going to be colder.'

I had met Stan a couple of times before but didn't quite know what to make of him. There is a hint of reserve in him that left me wondering if I'd ever really know him.

He's a real fly-fishing celebrity and in the same way I felt when I first headed out to fish with Alan, I was a little starstruck. Stan is sharper than most with a rod and with a pen. He is a cultured man, a writer and a thinking angler.

I'd interviewed him a couple of years earlier at a fly tying demonstration. I was filming it for a news report and as he deftly tied a Dunkeld Muddler, he opened his mouth, and his mind.

'A fly isn't just a work of art,' he pronounced as he snipped the deer-hair head into a mini shuttlecock.

'It is that all right, but it is more than that. It is a tool to be used. It is where art and function meet in the purest form.'

His thumb and index finger teased at the bright confection of fur and feather that he'd just conjured up in the vice for me.

Wow, I thought. This guy really gets it.

So I was nervous to be in the company of such a fine angler and a man who'd autographed my copy of his book: *Trout and Salmon Flies of Scotland.*

This was his first visit to Corrib and because I had control of the boat, I felt strongly that it was my responsibility to take him to where the fish were.

As it turned out, I needn't have worried. Fishing is a great leveller and ten hours in a boat together provides plenty of opportunity for fun.

It was a hailstorm that broke the ice. Stan had bought a poncho to keep the showers off. It went on over the head easily enough in the shop but he hadn't bargained for how it would perform in a howling gale.

As the hailstones bounced about the boat and stung any uncovered skin, the bespectacled Scotsman made a spectacle of himself. His head was firmly wedged into the sleeve and the nylon material flapped noisily in the wind.

Time and again he tried to pull it on and each attempt was funnier than the last. Swearing and struggling he pulled and tugged at the ridiculous thing. I laughed until the tears ran down my cheeks and my sides were sore.

Finally, just as the storm passed and the sun came out, his head popped into the hood. He emerged with his glasses half on, half off and wearing a startled expression. He laughed and cursed me and the impossible poncho.

We were fishing out the back of Inchiquin again when Stan cracked the trout code for the day. His size 14 buzzers were strung up near the surface by a bushy dry fly on the point. He was remarkably calm as the floating fly line swished off at breakneck speed, a spectacular wild brown on the business end. It was efficiently netted and knocked on the head with a brass priest - the last rites, performed quickly and cleanly.

I then saw him turn from fisherman into entomologist. The man from Fife carefully inserted a marrow spoon into the trout's stomach. The contents were dropped into a small white plastic dish and swished about with some water.

The fish had been gorging on the pupae and there were hundreds of them in the container.

'Do you see the silvery sheen on the body?' he asked as we peered into the soup. Some of them were still living and were indeed bathed in an iridescent skin over their wriggling bodies.

He laid the fish out, photographed it and we settled down to fish again.

Just before lunch, Stan snared another trout in similar

fashion and the same post mortem examination was observed with the same result. I only ever spoon fish when I don't know what they've been feeding on. It was obvious to me and to Stan that his trout were feeding hard on the buzzers but his inquisitive nature insisted on seeing the proof and perhaps finding fresh clues that might reap future benefits.

The day was punctuated by fish, the arc of brilliant rainbows and spectacular early spring weather. One of the bonuses of being out in a really open space is that you can see the rain or the sun coming, minutes before they hit.

We were near Birchall when Devenish Island disappeared under a silver curtain of hail. The wind stiffened and one by one the lake boats began to vanish. We watched the line of the storm approach as we zipped up our jackets and buttoned ourselves up in preparation for the inevitable.

'Do you hear that?' said Stan as he captured the moment on camera. We both listened to the low rumble of millions of hailstones crashing into the lake. It sounded like a train roaring along a track in the distance.

Closer and closer it raced, whipping the lake surface into white foam. When the storm hit, we sat huddled over, hoods up and hands tucked into pockets to avoid the painful sting of ice on cold, reddened skin.

The boat was full of slush when the storm passed. The air was cold and our breath condensed in the evening air.

'Let's go ashore for a cuppa,' said Stan. I threaded a path through some rocks and picked a sheltered shore on a narrow inlet. As we carried the picnic basket and flasks clear of the boat, Stan suddenly spotted a trout rise not far from the shore.

'I'm going to have a cast at that.' He chuckled as he reached for his rod. I took a short stroll around the whin bushes to see if there were any more rising fish.

'Darryl!' I heard the shout and turned to see the Scotsman holding a fine trout above his head. Stan was shaking it and laughing, like a big kid.

'That's one you caught earlier,' I bantered, thinking he was having me on. But when I reached him, Stan was grinning from ear to ear.

'I got him!' The fly-fishing celebrity, the angling author, the man I'd been nervous about sharing a boat with for the day, had gone. I was looking at a friend wearing dark-rimmed glasses and a great big smile.

'Wait till I tell the boys about this tonight!' '

'You can catch them from the boat AND the shore!' I giggled.

'I don't think it'll do much for my reputation', he said, recovering his composure.

'They'll just call me a bank angler.'

The Corrib was weaving her magic again, showing us for a short spell how generous she could be to men prepared to spend enough time in her company.

Trout were now rising freely in front of us, close to shore. It was time for the buzzers to hatch, 6pm our time, temperature and light dictating nature's time.

For nearly an hour we fished with hushed voices and

fluttering hearts. The telltale rings of water where the trout revealed themselves, silent targets for our tiny flies.

I fooled two trout in quick succession in the fading light. I touched their golden flanks and returned them while Stan proved he had one more secret up his sleeve.

Time and again his rod would lift and bend into a fish – but the renowned fly inventor had traded spots for stripes. He was catching PERCH.

Some fly fishermen despise them as a nuisance fish. They are blind to the beauty of these prickly customers – not Stan. He was as pleased as punch to catch them. We pored over the blood-red fins and spiked dorsal that sits high on a rough sandpaper skin.

They all weighed 1lb or more and each was considered beautiful enough for Stan to photograph it and gently return it to the shoal he'd found.

'You are the finest catcher of perch on Lough Corrib and a fine bank angler to boot,' I mocked as we packed the rods away in preparation for the half-hour journey back to the twinkling lights of civilisation.

My boat partner lit his pipe and smiled. I hope we live long enough to share a day like that again.

DAY FOUR

Cruising into Morgan's Bay, giving Molly's Rock a respectful berth, John Edwards and I were looking for shelter from a strong southerly wind that was threatening to turn into a full-blown gale.

The gentle Welshman with a boyish face framed by fine, gold-rimmed spectacles is a man of few words. His speech is slow and deliberate and so too are his movements. But John is no dozer. Now in his late fifties, there is still a sharpness in his eyes and, if anything, his passion for fly-fishing burns brighter now than when he fished for the Welsh International team in the 1980s.

A cock pheasant called for a mate as we approached the back of the bay. In the shelter of the shore, near the old stone wall that emerges from the trees, there was a short drift of about 100 metres allowing us to fish with epoxy buzzers.

The technique requires the boat to be drifting as slowly as possible so you can keep contact with the little flies as they fall. Beyond the glassy water close to shore, the wind would catch the broad side of the lough boat and push us along too quickly.

We saw a couple of trout feeding on the first drift but they were too far away from the boat, so I turned to repeat the process and was rewarded with a plump trout measuring thirteen inches. As I returned it, I didn't know it would be ten tough hours in horrendous conditions before I'd get another.

Much later, after a lunch eaten in the shelter of gorse bushes on a windswept island, I took time to watch John fishing. He has a one-off style reminiscent of how a Praying Mantis hunts. The rod was held high like the arm of a delicate crane. He made frequent very short casts and sat rigid, concentrating.

His eyes never strayed from the point where he expected his fly might be seized by a trout. We were drifting through a rocky area known as The Fuidges when I saw a blinding glint. A fish rolled sideways in four feet of water as it was met by a lightning response that any Praying Mantis would have been proud of.

'Got him!' muttered the canny Welshman, more to himself than to me. 'That size 14 Peter Ross has been very successful for me over the years.' His enjoyment had clearly loosened his tongue, but the delivery was still in the same, slow measured tone.

The afternoon was spent prospecting from place to place looking for trout and shelter and hoping for the wind to drop. On the way across the lake, into the teeth of the gale, we had to stop at the back of an island to bale the water out of the boat, before crossing to Bog Bay.

By rights we should have given up and gone back to the warmth and comfort of the B&B. The rest of our party had long since quit, but it never occurred to either of us to stop. I had a notion that if we just kept going we'd be rewarded and, as it turned out, I was right.

As dusk approached the wind dropped at last and the duckfly began to hatch. The trout were up and feeding confidently at the surface. We were both fishing a team of buzzers held up by a dry fly on the point – the 'washing line' as it's known in the trade.

But despite repeatedly covering feeding fish they absolutely refused to take our artificial pupae. It was 8pm when we each independently cut off the dry fly and added a fourth buzzer to the point of the cast, to allow them to fall naturally and deeper through the water.

We made the same calculation at the same time and hooked a fish at the same time. John had a ferocious take, which raced away towards the bow. The line cut the water with a swoosh as the trout careered off. A split second later, my rod was almost wrenched from my hand by a brownie weighing over 2lbs. The rod convulsed and the line raced from the coils on the floorboards with impressive speed.

Our reactions couldn't have been more different. John was his usual mild-mannered and methodical self. Traits put to good use with the Department of Agriculture in Wales. He'd given me a big grin earlier when he told me he counted sheep for a living.

I, of course, was shrieking in the stern. Shivering in the late evening chill, my rod shuddering and pulsing with life, I gabbled about how fabulous it was that we'd both managed to do the right thing at the right time.

'We're Kings of the Corrib!' I laughed as we netted the fish. 'We'll probably never forget this for the rest of our lives,' I insisted.

My companion raised a smile and I thought I'd finally shaken him out of his self-restraint.

'Yes, it was rather good,' said John. His deadpan delivery made me laugh like a lunatic.

In the morning I'd be making the long trek home. The thought hit me as we headed back to the B&B but I brushed it away. Now was the time to drink the last drop from the Corrib cup.

Night was stealing in as I steered a course towards civilisation, central heating and the rigid certainties of modern living.

The lake was calm and polished and reflected the moon and stars.

I don't know why, but I gave John a thumbs-up sign and smiled.

Sitting in the bow, his shoulders hunched against the cold, he grinned back like a Cheshire Cat.

We were both in the same place – off the map.

LICK THE
LIZARD

'Just pick it up and say something!' the director shouted from the far bank on the Grand Canal.

I laughed. Inside though, I was nervous as hell.

'We're running,' said Roger Ford-Hutchinson, indicating with that brisk phrase that the camera was burning tape.

Some directors call 'action!', others simply say 'in your own time, Darryl.' But the result is the same: you are on stage and the assembled crew is waiting for the performance.

But in the drama of fishing for TV, more often than not, there isn't any script and you simply make it up as you go along. Roger wanted my 'spontaneous' reaction to catching a fish – even though it had been caught minutes earlier and kept in the landing net at my feet while the camera position had been changed.

I looked down at the roach/bream hybrid, a drably coloured fish and the unremarkable result of an accidental
spawning between the two species.

'What am I going to say?' I thought, looking from the
gulping creature in my hands to the team of faces on the
far canal bank.

So I smiled, picked it up and said:

'There you are, a lovely hybrid. It just doesn't get any
better than that!'

Hardly poetry, but in that instant, sweating in the heat of
the midday sun near the sleepy village of Sallins, I had my
first taste of the pressure and pleasure of being the presenter of a fishing programme.

For the next few months, 'just pick it up and say something' became our catch phrase. It was a life-changing time
for me, the summer of 2001. It was when I began my
apprenticeship as a television presenter, making the *Coast
to Coast* series for BBC Northern Ireland and the Discovery
Home & Leisure channel.

The sun hardly stopped shining as we clocked up thousands of miles by road between Dublin and the Giant's
Causeway in search of fish and *Maeve*, the barge at the
centre of our adventure.

We spent three months on the road, criss-crossing Ireland, always tracking down our skipper, Liam Finnegan,
and hunting out our next fishing location and guest.

Most of the trips took us through the quintessentially
Irish town of Mullingar, with its wide main street and too
many pubs.

'It's in the middle of nowhere,' I mused apathetically from the back seat on one such trip.

'But it's close to everywhere,' quipped Roger, who may just have coined a new marketing slogan for the traffic-choked capital of the midlands.

Liam was constantly on the move too, negotiating locks and cruising ahead to be in position for the next filming day, when we'd create the illusion of a leisurely meander through the heart of Ireland.

The schedule was tight. We were always on the go, meeting up with him at quiet backwaters like Robertstown, Edenderry or Shannon Harbour every few days.

Liam is a big amiable man from Longford with a winning smile. He also has the patience of a saint. It took him weeks to steer the barge from the Liffey basin in Dublin, up the Grand Canal and then along the Shannon-Erne Waterway, finishing his part of the adventure at Belleek, in Fermanagh.

That was an epic 250-mile trip but Liam was forced to sail many more miles than that, due to the demands of doing it for the television.

I saw him smile thinly many times because he was constantly having to turn the boat and go back as we needed to film the barge from different vantage points. Just as often, it was down to me, because I had messed up my lines in a PTC – the dreaded Piece to Camera.

These links where I delivered scripted lines straight to camera were invariably choreographed to coincide with our passage under a bridge, leaving a lock or going past a landmark. Each failed attempt required Liam to go back and the whole thing to be set up again. It was no mean feat for him, considering the canal is only a little wider than the barge.

There are so many memories from that summer. But there are two key ones. The dominant and most compelling is fishing in fabulous places I'd never been before, sometimes for fish I'd never caught before, but always with the best anglers in the country of Ireland. The other is much more painful.

From the outset, I surprised myself because I didn't know until then that I had a talent for talking about the fish. Excitement and enthusiasm are as infectious as laughter and my passion for the sport and the fish were, and are, plain to see. I loved getting my hands on them and trying to connect with the audience down that cold, black lens.

I was always absolutely at ease, totally happy and comfortable when I was catching for the camera. I could ad lib all day long, but there are other skills that are as least as important in telling the story on telly and that's where the pain kicked in.

At the start of filming, I had big problems performing the formal PTCs. In trying to deliver the script in a conversational, chatty way, I found I couldn't get the words out. I got tongue tied under pressure and the early part of the adventure was blighted for me because of it.

Years of working as a news journalist on radio and TV had not prepared me for this. In that world, you can get away with writing the facts, trotting them off as a reporter but never really putting yourself on camera.

Here the performance needed to be softer, more inti-
mate and rounded – just like acting. I had to walk and talk,
hit a mark and talk again. Being more than a talking head
was very different indeed and it stretched my ability to the
end of the elastic.

At the start I dreaded the days on the barge when we'd
have to travel long distances and knock off several of these
links across several different programmes one after
another. The problems were all in my head of course,
because by the end of the journey I had finished the first
stage of my apprenticeship and could manage to perform
the script like the words had just occurred to me.

Looking back, I can remember the exact moment when
it became a problem. It was the first day of filming, in
Dublin, when I discovered TV presenter's hell. Perched at
the front of the barge, I had to introduce myself and give a
cheery mission statement for the series.

All I had to say was: 'Hello and welcome to *Coast to Coast*,
an angling adventure across Ireland. I'm Darryl Grimason, a
mad keen fisherman, and on this trip if it's got fins, I'll be fishing for it. Our journey begins here, on the River Liffey in
Dublin. Out there *(pointing down stream)* is the Irish Sea and
ahead of us are the sea locks to the Grand Canal, the gateway
to fabulous fishing as we go, coast to coast.'

I just couldn't get the words out in one take, even though
I'd written them myself and learned them off. Over and over
again I tried and time and again I stumbled and fluffed.

Liam was a long way from me, at the tiller in the stern

and the camera crew was in another boat. I felt exposed and alone. Roger's vision for the shot was that the barge and the camera boat would circle each other so that, as I spoke, the background would constantly change, revealing a panoramic view of the city from the river.

Each time I failed to do it, both boats had to reposition. Allowing for wind, tide and a slow-moving barge, it all took far more time than was budgeted for. All eyes were on me and I was conscious that I was holding everyone up. Each failure put more pressure on me and added to the sense of impatience I could feel radiating from behind the camera.

The weight of the entire enterprise was pressing down on me, making me shrink inside. Relentlessly it went on, over and over until finally, at last, I managed to get the words out.

I didn't even do it well in the end and I still wince when I see it. I felt like a complete and abject failure. My confidence had been shattered within the first hours of filming.

Life has a way of ambushing you at times, when even simple things can become impenetrable if you think about them too much. I'd been preparing for that moment for months and yet, when it arrived, I wasn't ready. It got to me and left me feeling useless.

There is nowhere to hide when you are on camera and it's going wrong. It is a very lonely place.

So my response to the demand that I 'just pick it up and say something' a couple of days later was a tiny step towards rehabilitation.

So too was the fact that there was no pressure that day because the fish had read the script – the canal was full of them. Thanks to Dave McNeice, an Irish international angler, and a wizard with a carbon fibre roach pole, we caught coarse fish all day long.

Dave was a presenter's dream. He was bright, articulate and could keep the banter going. He had the fish eating out of his hand. Golden rudd with blood red fins, curiously coloured rudd/bream hybrids, perch and even tench, they were all there for the taking. He picked them from the shallow water and taught me to do the same with a tiny float, maggots and a ten-metre pole. It was simplicity itself.

We'd arrived early in the morning, with the last frost of the spring still clinging to the bankside grass. It was a gloriously clear May Day bank holiday and the air was fresh and sweet.

'Do you think we have a chance of a tench today?' I asked.

'You never know,' he said. 'There's a big head of tench in this part of the canal but it might be a wee bit early in the season and a bit bright today,' he added, giving himself some wriggle room.

And when I did catch my first tench early in the afternoon, I forgot all about my failings as a TV presenter. I just struggled with the fish, amazed by it's brute power and ability to stretch the yellow elastic in the pole to the far distance.

'It's heading for Prosperous,' I said, standing up and walking along the towpath towards the next village like a man being pulled by a dog on a leash.

It took ages to subdue but eventually, when it was safely

in the net, the tench glistened like stained glass from an old church window. I took in everything at once – the ruby red eyes, tiny scales and the thick muscle wrist on the enormous tail.

It was once known as the Doctor's Fish, because its viscous slime is said to have healing properties. Catching it was a tonic for my nerves. I shook hands with Dave, thanked him for teaching me how to catch such a fabulous specimen, and entirely forgot I was on camera. All I was was a fisherman who'd captured a rare and exciting fish and who was elated by the encounter.

I was the new boy in a small team who'd all known each for years making programmes for BBC Northern Ireland. The *Coast to Coast* series had two producer/directors, Roger and Carole Johnston, whose idea the series was.

They would produce and direct five each of the ten-part series. They'd also edit the episodes they directed. And just to add to the workload, they would film some of the scenes with a second camera as well as organising the logistics of filming with Liam, along with a hundred other details. Both are amazingly talented, versatile people.

The crew was sharp too. Seamas McCracken has quick, hungry eyes. His gaze takes all of you in at once, in a fast scan. They are always inquisitive, always looking for another angle. This hard working lensman is among the best cameramen I've worked with. His friend and our colleague Derek Hehir is a top class sound recordist. The lads were a tight knit exclusive team that shared a white Volkswagen van, and an irreverent sense of humour.

They travelled and operated as a team within the team.

All of them loved the days aboard *Maeve*, cruising the forgotten byways. Roger confesses it was the happiest summer's work he's ever had. And apart from the early frustrations of having to work around my inexperience, all of us have great memories of the trip.

For my part, I was always looking forward to the next fishing stop-off. Great days, like the time we captured bream as big as bin lids with Liam Kane at Inny Bay on Lough Ree, the Lake of Kings.

I caught neon orange and blue cockoo wrasse in Donegal Bay, big plaice on the sand under the Giant's Causeway and wild brown trout in Lough Erne. The fishing was stunning and the fish were queuing up for a starring role on television. I managed to squeeze in a lifetime's fishing adventure in that long, hot summer.

There were so many good days that it's impossible to write about them all. But the pike fishing was phenomenally good with Jimmy Scotson, on Monalty Lake near Carrickmacross. I managed a 19 pounder – my second heaviest. Derek and Roger even managed to catch their first pike when we stopped filming. That was a very happy day.

And again, with David Overy on Lough Glore in the midlands. This cultured Dubliner is cucumber cool, but with an intense passion for our biggest freshwater predators. We managed an 18lb plus pike for the camera and caught lots of other double figure pike – few of which appeared on screen.

David and I were having a ball while Seamas, Carole

and Derek were stuck in the mud with their boatman at the far end of the lake. Access to the lough had been a problem but that little detail illustrated another key rule of television: If it doesn't happen on camera, it didn't happen!

We met loads of interesting and even strange people on our travels. Lough Glore had an odd feel about it, cradled in the bog, near the bellybutton of Ireland.

It was the year of fishing and land restrictions following the outbreak of foot-and-mouth disease in the North. We had to get special permission to cross the fields to the lake and when we arrived, several of the locals were there, curious to see the film crew.

While setting up the rods, I spotted a beautiful green-eyed child with lemon blonde hair. It was curled in tight, natural ringlets. She was about three years old and was nursing a burned hand. It was badly scalded and blistered in an accident, her mother told me.

'She'll be all right now, I got the charm from the man up the road,' she said, without a hint of irony or self-consciousness.

Us folk from the Big Smoke looked at each other in disbelief as she explained. Apparently there was a man who had developed special powers because he had – wait for it – licked a lizard! What species, colour or size this reptile was, history does not relate. But given that the countryside is not awash with them, this creature must indeed have been an oddity.

And given that rarity, the gift of healing was made even harder to obtain because it had to be a chance encounter.

You had not to go looking for the reptile, said the woman, speaking with a thick midlands twang and a matter-of-fact delivery. No, it had to find you and you, as far as I could understand, had to lick the lizard to become the charmer of warts, scalds and other ills.

I swear the duelling banjo and guitar from the film *Deliverance* were playing softly in the distance. But maybe I just dreamed what could easily have been a scene from *Father Ted*. I recently asked Carole if I'd been hallucinating but she confirmed it had been a real conversation with a real woman. It takes all sorts ...

I wonder how good the man with the charm would have been at encouraging shy fish to show up for the camera. It didn't happen that often but, occasionally, the fish forsook me.

As a result, there were always off-screen decisions with on-screen implications for me, like the time we tried fishing for the notoriously difficult wild brown trout on Lough Ennell, near Mullingar.

Local fisheries officer Pat McDonnell and I rode out a storm on the lough in bright sunshine in late June and never saw a fish all day.

My 'reward' for this was the added pressure of having to secure some wild trout for the programme, this time from the River Brosna, in County Offaly.

Early one morning, Pat called at the hotel and we put together a convoy, him leading the way, Carole and me in the hired Ford Galaxy and Seamas and Derek following in the VW van.

We stopped at a big open stretch of the river and my heart sank. I had an eight-foot rod that throws a number four line and I was looking at a piece of water that needed a ten-footer and a number seven. It was like being asked to drive a golf ball 350 yards with a putter.

There was a cold wind and a total absence of rising trout. It looked hopeless. Pat jumped into the car and led our convoy at speed down country lanes, stopping at various holes in the hedge to peer at the water, always with the same result - no feeding fish.

Finally, we crossed Belmont Bridge, at a stretch that runs cheek by jowl with the Grand Canal. Instantly, I knew our mission was now possible. It was like the Upper Bann at Banbridge, all broken water, pools and glides. And most importantly of all, there were fish – admittedly small ones – but trout feeding in the current.

I tied on a size 16 grey midge and began casting upstream. Carole, Seamas and Derek were well behind me, filming the stalk when I caught the first of several lovely little trout. They were all about eight inches long, and looked identical, like peas in a pod.

One by one I spotted the spotted predators calmly breaking the surface as they nipped the miniscule flies from the surface and one by one I caught them with precision and practised guile.

Penned in by my three colleagues, casting the flies clear of them and over the fish I loved every minute of it. Here at last I was doing what I knew how to do and doing it with absolute certainty.

Soon the procession of four pairs of feet, three of them unused to walking an uneven riverbed, took their toll on the fishing and the trout stopped rising.

'We need another fish,' said Carole. It was the first time I recall her saying it, but it was not the last. She is merciless in her pursuit of that last fish for the camera.

Anyway, map in hand, we went back to the wagons and raced off down the country lanes again, all for one more fish. We found none. An hour later we were back at Belmont Bridge, the river had forgotten us and the wee fish were rising again.

My three colleagues stayed on the bridge and filmed while I waded upstream, hunting for the last trout. When I caught the final tiddler, I could not have been happier if I'd just landed a whopper. Minnows and monsters, they're all the same to me. That day is one of my happiest memories of the entire series.

All the fishermen we worked with were acutely aware of the pressure they were under to catch fish on camera. Each was a class act, selected from the thousands of anglers around Ireland because they were the best available. Fishermen like Damien Maddock, who's fished for his country many times.

It was 8am when we arrived at Galmoylestown lake in the midlands, for a day's carp fishing. My bearded guest had been on the lake for hours already and was putting a carp into his keep net as we walked along the shore to meet him.

Damien was so uptight about the filming that he had been unable to sleep. Worried that he might blank, the quietly spoken Dubliner drove up to the midlands and had begun fishing before first light.

And it looked like he'd caught every carp in the lake. His keep net was full to bursting point with at least thirty big fat carp crammed inside.

The sun was shining, the sky was blue and it looked like we were in for a fantastic day's fishing. But fate can be cruel. Damien didn't know it, but that carp he'd caught as we approached was the last one he would catch all day. It was as if someone had flicked a switch and every carp in the lake refused to co-operate.

We sat, for hours on the shore, bombarding the area around our floats with great handfuls of maggots. The long periods of inactivity were broken by an occasional false promise as the waggler floats dipped under.

But each time a tiny rudd would be reeled in. The carp had deserted us. Afternoon turned to evening and the sun began its descent behind the trees on the far shore. The light was fading and with it, our chances.

Damien and I sat silently, staring at the orange-topped floats in the middle of the silky smooth lake. We were willing them to go under but still unable to believe what was happening.

I'd become increasingly desperate. I knew Seamas and Derek were due to pack up for the day at 7.30pm. I could see them checking the time, thinking about dinner and a pint in Mullingar. All I wanted was a fish. I was in exactly the same state of mind as when I was a boy, mentally pleading for five more minutes, for just one fish.

I was also personally disappointed because I'd never caught a carp, never even fished for one before and this might be my only chance to do it.

Despite the wait, Damien was confident we would get a fish, if we waited long enough. 'They'll start to feed when the sun goes off the water,' he told me.

And sure enough, at exactly 7.30pm a miracle happened. My float dipped, lifted and then slid under. Instinctively I lifted the rod and felt the weight of a big fish surge away as it felt the hook.

In sheer excitement and disbelief, I stood and shouted: 'Fish!' The long wait was over. The adrenalin was coursing though my veins, leaving me breathless and making my legs shake and my knees weak.

Damien was at my shoulder. 'It's a good fish,' he said. 'Careful, play it gently.'

I did so but could not believe the power of the creature I'd just hooked. With only 4lb breaking strain line, I could not afford to bully or force it. Time and again it tore line off as it raced around the shallow lake and all the time, as I shared my joy with the camera, I was terrified.

'Please God, don't let it get away,' I kept thinking.

By the time Damien netted the fish I was so wound up, so relieved, so grateful that the most important guest of the programme had finally arrived that I totally lost the plot.

I was so close to tears that my voice was several pitches higher than usual and my eyes filled up. I had to blink just to see straight.

This was the first time I realised that the camera makes a

huge difference. It heightens the highs because each fish is much more important than on a private fishing trip. But it also deepens the low points, because there is so much riding on hooking a fish.

The American writer Zane Grey wrote in his epic, *Tales of Swordfish and Tuna*, that: 'To catch a fish is not all of fishing.' It's the philosophical truth all right – but on TV to catch a fish is everything.

And that carp, at that time, meant the world to me. My hands were shaking like a leaf as I bent over the landing net to pick her out.

'Thank you Damien, thank you,' I said, my voice quivering with emotion.

With the camera on me, in the fading light of a long and difficult day, I stood centre stage and spoke from the heart: 'This is so sweet, I've been here over eight hours and I was just beginning to doubt myself. I invested so much of myself here today. I was just beginning to doubt myself, but that's what fishing is, suddenly your float goes under and you are into a real quality carp – I'm not going to fish again tonight. This fish is enough for me today.'

With the camera turned off, I actually jumped for joy.

'I thought you were really going to cry,' Seamas said to me later.

'That was great television,' said Carole. 'I'm going to run all of that.'

It was then that I felt my elation turn very quickly to deep embarrassment. I had just bared my soul on camera. I felt naked and silly and sure that anyone who saw me make such a spectacle of myself over an 8lb carp would laugh at me.

As it turned out, no one has ever even mentioned that scene to me, one way or the other. In an odd way I suppose it showed just how deeply fish can move anglers. But that night, I promised myself that I'd never again allow that much of me, the real me, to go on public display.

At that point, I could not separate myself, the private me, from the very public persona of the presenter. Years down the line, there is clear blue water between the two. You have to develop a split personality, allowing the performer to take over on camera and the real you to walk away and watch 'him' in the edit suite later.

Tears very nearly flowed again at Carnroe weir on the Lower River Bann, the day I caught my first salmon on the fly. I'd always been unlucky with salmon. Sure I'd caught plenty of them on the spinner, on the River Moy, between Ballina and Foxford in wildest County Mayo, but the water was never right when I was chasing them on the fly.

'You should have been here last week … the river will be perfect tomorrow': the advice is always the same and the time is never right.

I'd endured lots of that privately when I met Tommy McCutcheon, at the start of a day's fishing and filming for *Coast to Coast*. Tommy's a tackle dealer with a shop on Belfast's Sandy Row and a mighty man with a double-handed salmon rod. It was first light when we waded into the shallows and a thick mist floated eerily across the river. I put my faith in him and my fly in the water.

In the hours that followed I saw more wild Atlantic salmon in one place than I had in my entire life. They pitched and rolled – hundreds of them in the current. Tommy showed how it was done, catching two with consummate ease.

Like all trout anglers, I could not resist the temptation to strike when for the first time ever, a salmon grabbed my fly. I made contact for only a fraction of a second before the fish was lost.

I knew I had to allow a loop of line slide from my fingers before lifting the rod because the fish take the lure and turn away before closing their mouth. But excitement and the habits of a lifetime are hard to disobey and I messed it up.

I was upset and beginning to doubt if I'd ever get another chance when another fish snatched my Curry's Red Shrimp.

This time the line peeled out, I lifted and felt the fish bang and thump the line with his tail but said nothing. I could not believe it had happened but I wanted to make sure the salmon was really on, before I shouted: 'Fish!'

When that fresh-run grilse was hooked at the tail of the pool, it was a fishing ambition fulfilled. I was gripped by that fish in exactly the same way the carp had moved me but when I heard my voice change – I mentally stepped back and pulled on the presenter's mask.

'That's a dream in that net,' I said, going completely over the top. 'I've dreamed that dream for years and there's real emotion in that.

'This is my Holy Grail, my miracle – a platinum fish straight from the sea. In my fishing life, I have never been happier,' I said, and I meant every word of it.

'Did I hear a wee tremor in the voice?' inquired Seamas when we'd finished filming, a wicked smirk playing at the corner of his mouth.

'No tears this time,' I said, holding out my trembling hands, palms downwards.

I'd managed to show how happy and touched by the experience I really was, but still kept faith with myself. The feeling was personally and professionally very sweet indeed.

'This day will live with me for a lifetime,' I told the audience. It has and so too has the experience and the privilege of fishing and travelling to make that series.

By the end of filming, sitting on the hexagonal stones of the Giant's Causeway, I had goose bumps all over when I delivered my last PTC in the golden light of a glorious sunset.

It was an emotional farewell and I was genuinely sorry that I had delivered my final Piece to Camera. I took several goes at it as usual, but by then I was so much a part of the team that I was comfortable with them, even when I couldn't do something.

I had learned by then to be easier on myself when I didn't reach the impossibly high standards I set myself. As we climbed into the cars at the end of a journey that had been a road to discovery for me, I was determined to keep travelling – I knew there was more fishing adventure out there for me. I was determined to make sure that I'd get another chance.

BE CAREFUL
WHAT YOU
WISH FOR

Being a fishaholic is the world's most popular addiction. There are millions of us out there, hooked on fishing. Find any riverbank or lake where fins are in supply and the extent of the epidemic is obvious. Lost souls can be found, wearing an absent look and staring at the water in a trance-like state.

Camouflaged in green, they hide behind umbrellas, stalk under bushes and sneak about on the water's edge. Each is hoping to score a quick carp, or bag a net full of bream. Surrounded by mountains of tackle, the lucky ones sport benevolent smiles. Those with all the gear and no idea, sit slouched in despondency until they get their fishy fix.

I count myself among them. It sounds like you should stand up and declare it in the best traditions of self-help groups: 'My name is Darryl Grimason and I'm a fishaholic! I'm an angling junkie who's not too choosy about which mind-expanding fish I get a high from.'

I have a preference for predators, but I'm not that picky about how I get my hands on them. When there's a craving for wild brown trout, the best hit is on a dry fly but I'm no purist. For perch I'll fish a spinner or a worm and for pike, I prefer moving lures – but the effects of a specimen over 20lbs remain untried, by this fishaholic at least.

As a rule of thumb, the bigger the fish, the bigger the kick but unlike other harmful addictions, this worldwide phenomenon is largely benign. It's loaded with life-enhancing experiences and at its best, can wash body and mind with an enormous rush of well being.

On the downside, it is incurable, selfish and costly. The habit eats time, money and sometimes relationships, as some divorced fishaholics can testify.

Some get it worse than others and in my experience, the big fish specialists have it worst of all. Theirs is the purest drug: they target only the rare, large fish in any given species. These macho men (I have not yet heard of a woman specimen hunter) give themselves over entirely to the quest.

They are on the extreme fringe of the fishaholic world, but their motivation is a shared ideal. The desire to catch a big fish is shot through every angler like lettering runs through a bar of seaside rock. It doesn't matter if you pick up a rod only once in your life, or once every day, you absolutely WILL want to cast to a monster.

The Angler's Prayer says it all:

Lord, grant that I may catch a fish so big that even I,
When speaking of it afterwards, may
Have no need to lie.
Amen.

Therein lies nearly everything you need to know about how we brothers of the angle think about big fish. They are more elusive than a hole-in-one, a Royal Flush or the pot of gold at the end of the rainbow.

The very fact that they are so rare, so difficult to catch makes them all the more desirable. Until I'd reached the ripe old age of forty, I'd seen but never caught a really big fish. That is sadly the experience of most average anglers, yet I have always been fascinated by the thought of them.

Since my earliest fishing addiction I dreamed of very heavy fish. Over the years I devoured books and stories about them and the men who wrestled immense creatures out on the blue horizon. I found them in Ernest Hemingway's *The Old Man and The Sea*, Peter Benchley's *Jaws*, Herman Melville's *Moby Dick*, and the incredible tales of giant fish written by Zane Grey.

I wanted to find that world of epic adventure and great drama in Ireland but I wanted to do it for TV. I had no idea what I was taking on when I dreamed up a plan to make a television fishing series exclusively about big predatory fish. I had enough excellent contacts around the island to know in my heart that it was possible and, at the time, that was all the encouragement I needed.

After my experience making *Coast to Coast*, I had evolved into a fishaholic who'd overdosed on optimism and the desire to hook my dreams on camera. It was both brave and stupid to want it because the odds against catching the big ones are always against the angler, even when time is not an issue. On TV time is money, money equals budget and budget equals limited time fishing.

The big fish equation also comes down to simple maths. There are always going to be many more small fish than monsters and the few large fish there are didn't get that way by throwing themselves onto the first hook dangled in front of them. To catch them, you need knowledge, skill, stubborn, obsessive determination and that incalculable ingredient, luck.

I knew we had some huge fish living very close to our shores but I also knew that most people had no idea that they were there. I believed they would be surprised and amazed by what swims right up to our doorstep. My instinct said they'd be bowled over by seeing them.

As the vision crystallised, I wrote the following proposal for a series.

BIG SIX

The ultimate hunt for top predators in Irish waters - the big game-hunter's wish list! You don't have to travel to the Gulf of Mexico or Great Barrier Reef to find fish that pull like an express train they're off the Irish coast and in our lakes and rivers.

The star of the *Coast to Coast* fishing series Darryl Grimason will target the top dogs - toothy critters with attitude.

Big Six will also tell the story of fishermen obsessed with their target species – hearing tales of monstrous fish that pulled boats to the horizon; of the joy of success and heartbreak of the ones that got away.

THE TARGET

Blue Sharks are a turbo-charged torpedo and a prized fighting fish. Late summer off the West Coast they gather, crunching their way through the huge mackerel shoals.

Giant Bluefin Tuna – the biggest sportfish in Irish waters. Specimens up to 1,000lbs are increasingly caught by anglers in the bays around Donegal in September. Strapped into a fighting chair and chasing these predators in a purpose-built boat is a high in itself.

Conger eels - cave dwellers with a dark look and a mood to match - in the wreckage of sunken ships, they grow frighteningly big.

Common skate – of uncommon size. Huge specimens over 100lbs that 'hoover' up large fish over the sandy bed of the Atlantic Ocean.

Pike – the grandmother of them all – top dog in lakes and rivers with a mouth to match – nothing less than 20lbs will do.

Ferox trout – trolling for spotted terrors over 20lbs in Lough Corrib – they're the most ferocious brown trout – cannibalistic, always hungry with head and jaws evolved for crunching their prey.

Pulse-racing, adrenalin-pumping action for the armchair angler! A six-part series for BBC NI. Written and presented by Darryl Grimason. Produced and directed by Carole Johnston.

With some fine-tuning and help from Carole, without whose considerable talents the series could not have been made, we submitted it to the executives at Broadcasting House. The suits in Belfast were intrigued. We were invited to make a pitch, to convince them to spend licence payers' money on making the series.

The pair of us walked into the boardroom and wowed the execs with a tape measure and pictures of the Irish record Giant Bluefin Tuna. We were excited and nervous as we took it in turns to preach the gospel of *Big Six*.

'This is the length of a Giant Bluefin Tuna weighing 1,000lbs,' I said, standing ten feet away from Carole, who was holding the other end of the measuring tape.

'And this is the fish,' said Carole, producing a picture of Adrian Molloy, Ireland's top tuna skipper, looking like a mini-man standing beside an enormous fish.

We sold them a safari. Instead of the Big Five in Africa, we were hunting Ireland's Big Six. We offered them a white-knuckle ride and told them the series would be brave, ambitious and unique.

'What if you don't catch the fish?' asked one of the panel members.

'We'll have plenty of archive footage and we'll film some of the species in aquariums, so you will at least see the fish,' said Carole.

'We'll catch them,' I said with absolute certainty and absolutely no idea how difficult it would be to keep my word.

When the people at the top said we could make it, I was overjoyed. Carole had a much better grasp of what we'd taken on and of the difficulties that lay ahead.

'Now all we have to do is make it,' she said wryly.

Be careful what you wish for, the old saying goes, because you might get it. It's great advice because the series turned out to be the toughest thing anyone on the team had ever done for television.

We promised it would be memorable: it turned out to be unforgettable.

Our brief was not to make programmes that appealed only to anglers. We had to make a series that would also be watched by a wider audience and that brought with it additional challenges.

Carole constantly asked: 'How can we make this different, how can we make it better?' As the writer and presenter of the series I was inspired to look for the answers.

The results were great fun. We'd come up with lots of ideas and Carole would make them happen. I drove a Ferrari around the Nutts Corner racetrack in County Antrim, to illustrate the speed and power of the Giant Bluefin Tuna. I flew a kite as big as a parachute to show the great fighting strength of the Common Skate. The Irish Air Corps flew us around the Donegal coast to spot tuna the way they do in America and I got to talk to myself on screen, using trick photography.

Those parts of the jigsaw were the easy ones to find and place. All we had to do was make the telephone calls, agree arrangements and people would make things happen. But you can't phone a fish and book it for a starring role in a TV series. We had no control over our slippery guests, the element they live in, or the weather. That made *Big Six* incredibly difficult to make.

Never work with children or animals, the saying goes. I now believe that big fish should be added to the list. Once you put 'Big' in the title, small just don't count.

Blood, sweat and tears were shed on the adventure. We never knew when or if the fish would turn up. Every day was a journey into the unknown. We booked the best skippers and fished with people with a proven track record of success with the big fish we wanted. We picked the top venues, the most productive times and the latest equipment, yet the unpredictability of the hunt repeatedly threw our plans into chaos.

The battle to find the fish came out slightly ahead of the constant fight with seasickness. Carole and I had not taken account of human frailty when we made our plans.

'If you can manage lunch any day it's a triumph,' said Carole, who experimented with every anti-seasickness tablet known to modern medicine. Our leader also used magnetic bracelets, ginger biscuits and a host of other home-grown cures.

'When you hear the rattle of the cool box lid, you know it's going to be a good day,' she mused over dinner one evening. It was the truth.

On the first and only time Seamas succumbed to the sea, he confessed that he ran from the boat to the car in Ballycastle to see the physical effect.

'I had always heard that you turn green,' he said.

'I wanted to see how green I really was. With so much sea fishing to do I could see the whole series looming ahead of me. But the next time, when I wasn't sick, I was elated.'

Our colleagues in Belfast thought we were having a ball, gallivanting about the island all summer, looking for a few fish. They had no idea and neither did the audience, which is how it should be.

The trials and tribulations of making *Big Six* are neither here nor there to the man, woman or child sitting in front of the telly. They rightly only get to see the best bits, to be carried away on a smiling adventure, to get lost in the wild for half an hour from the comfort of their living room.

That is partly why I wanted to tell people about the stuff that happened behind the scenes. The good and bad experiences that Carole, Seamas, Derek and I shared along the road to making the series.

You can see how people thought we were on a cake-walk. We were indeed incredibly lucky to escape the desk, to be travelling to amazing places and in the company of great characters. The real stars of the show were the fish, the men and women obsessed with catching them and the island itself. Their stories were compelling but so too was the backdrop against which their tales were told. The Irish coast and our great lakes are world-class filming locations. We live in an astonishingly beautiful landscape.

For me there are two great 'fishy' moments that dominate my best recollections of *Big Six* but neither one involved me actually catching a fish. My number one, beats-the-rest-by-a-mile memory was the day we spent off the Donegal coast, being surrounded by gannets and Giant Bluefin Tuna. You can read about it later.

The other big one for me was the capture of a Blue Shark weighing 127lbs. Portrush angler Seamas Doherty caught it at the annual Shark Festival, in Donegal.

The fish was a primal force to be reckoned with and summed up everything I imagined *Big Six* would be. Seamas fought her for forty five minutes, during which she made terrifying runs, which sent spray flying from his multiplier reel. His wiry frame shook and jerked as the open ocean shark rolled and raced away.

He stood on the deck of the Bonito charter boat slugging it out with her while I commentated on a fight that could just as easily have been taking place off the East Coast of America. I was living out a fantasy.

Our team was so well drilled that we also managed to get stunning film of the creature as she fought to throw the hook. Normally fish are beaten by the time the underwater camera is dropped in but on this occasion, Carole left Seamas and I to do our job on deck while she recorded the power of a big shark in full flight.

I'd included Blue Sharks in the series because ever since I read *Jaws* when I was 12, I'd always wanted to see and to touch a real shark. Ireland's western coast is on the migratory route north for the juvenile females each summer. They are not too difficult to catch, if you can find them.

When Seamas's prize was hauled on board, it was seven feet long and worthy of the name Shark! It was the heaviest fish of the festival and one of the biggest caught in Ireland that season. She possessed such terrible beauty, with her ebony eyes, cobalt back and snow white belly, that I actually got goose bumps as I ran my hands over her rough skin.

Derek loved it: 'I wasn't prepared for seeing sharks but when we released that one and saw it swimming under the boat I suddenly realised how they got their name. It was electric blue,' he said.

But for every high there were plenty of lows. *Big Six* was at the same time a blessing and a curse to make and by the end of filming, everyone on the team was glad to walk away from it.

'It was not a relaxing series to make,' said Seamas, who describes himself as being 'reluctantly from Ballymena.' He is the stoic sort who just gets on with the job. 'I was glad it was over but would not have missed doing it.'

Derek's opinion was stronger still: 'I remember feeling great that it was over but even better that we didn't have to go back.'

Carole still shudders when we talk about it, so much so that she can't identify a single best moment.

'I cannot put into words how mentally tough it was. I spent too much time worrying, bobbing about in a boat. Every single minute I was sitting there thinking, we're burning time. There was no control and for someone with my nature, it was the wrong project,' she said.

I included these comments so that you know there was a personal price to be paid and not just by me. The following chapters are snapshots in time, told from my perspective mainly as an angler. I don't want to dwell too heavily on the negative parts now but without them, there is no context for understanding how amazing it was when everything went right. Without failure there can be no success. I didn't understand that properly until I had to swallow several bitter pills.

You must also understand that each story is written separately but in real life, they were running side by side. At one point in the middle of filming we had three successive trips where the fish failed to show up. I was seriously depressed as we moved from Ferox trout to Conger eels and then pike without success. My colleagues were reduced to playing 'I Spy' to put the days in and teased that we could always rename it *Big Three*.

Having said all that, *Big Six* is in my opinion great TV for the very reason that it stretched all of us to the limit and beyond. Had it been easier to make, it would not have been as exciting. Jeopardy is a concept that producers usually have to build into shows, on ours it was present in every frame.

There is another point I'd like to make. None of the fish we caught was killed. We returned them to the water alive. The need for active conservation cropped up time and again during the making of the series because our target fish are under pressure in the wild.

Their fates are mirrored by many of the other great predators, like the wolf or tiger. Sharks are possibly the most successful flesh eaters the world has ever seen (after us that is) and yet they are in most danger. Many of the Blue Sharks we found off the north-west coast can end up being 'finned', a gruesome practice performed on an industrial scale around the world. Commercial long lines are baited and set and when these elegant eating machines are caught, all their valuable fins are sliced off. The living torso is dumped overboard. The parts are destined for the sharkfin soup trade in the Far East. It's responsible for the death of tens of millions of sharks every year.

The blues that visit our seas are part of that global problem because they roam so widely. One fish was tagged off Loop Head in County Clare but turned up 4,000 miles away off Venezuela. Others have been recaptured in the Gulf of Mexico and much further north, off Long Island.

Another great pelagic hunter, the Giant Bluefin Tuna, has also experienced a huge drop in numbers over recent decades; Common Skate are now an officially endangered species. There is new evidence that one of our most common coastal fish, the Conger eel, is also in decline.

Although plentiful, pike are slaughtered with a demonic fervour both officially and unofficially in Ireland. They are considered a 'foreign' fish by the authorities, a political view used to justify the destruction of countless thousands of them every year.

Killing Ferox trout in order to have them stuffed and mounted on the wall is also having an effect. You'll read later how difficult it was for us to catch one for the series. I personally believe the trade in such trophies was a factor and that their numbers are dwindling. I was told privately by men with expert knowledge and in a position to know that they share my view.

What a travesty to think that more than 10,000 years after these trout swam in on the melt waters of the last Ice Age, anglers might help them swim into the history books.

The series only lightly touched on that bigger picture but it's sobering to think that it might be impossible to make the same show in, say, twenty years time because the fish may not be there.

In the end, I'm just thankful I got the chance to do it. Lots of those who watched *Big Six* stopped me on the street and told me how much they loved it. Oddly, about half of them were women. The conversation would usually begin: 'I have no interest in fishing, but I love your show…' I took particular satisfaction in that because it meant we had achieved our goal.

The presenter always gets the credit but any project is only as good as the sum of the talents that make it. Derek Hehir and Seamas McCracken consistently turned their lives upside down to race off at a moment's notice to some stormy shore in search of the invisible. They did the impossible with good grace, great panache and absolute professionalism.

Back at base, Dolores Shields cut the series brilliantly from the comfort of her edit suite but it was all managed, nursed, worried over and pulled together by the best, most gifted producer I know. Carole Johnston's single-minded determination not to be beaten by the fish, the weather or anything else beyond our power helped drag us through.

The entire venture rested on her slim shoulders. It nearly drove her to distraction but Carole's creative fingerprints are all over the finished product. I owe her a debt for giving me my start as a television presenter on *Coast to Coast* AND for realising my wishes for *Big Six*.

We are all intensely proud of what we did and, despite everything, the series was a success. It won awards in the UK and Ireland and blew away the myth that fishing is a brainless, boring pastime practised by creaking old men in cloth caps.

But of all the kind, complimentary things people have said to me, the best, funniest, sharpest insight came in the following quote from a woman who doesn't fish.

'It was Moby Dick every night!' she said. I'll settle for that.

IN SEARCH OF
LEVIATHANS

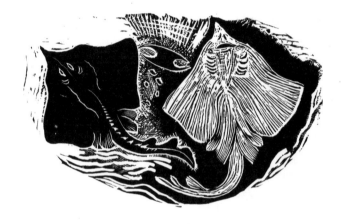

'Enjoy every minute of it,' said Carole as we entered the Central Bar in the middle of Ballycas-tle. 'It's going to be over before we know it,' she said and I nodded eagerly.

It was a Saturday night and the bar was heaving with punters. We entered the pub and disappeared into a fog of cigarette smoke, loud chatter and guitar music from the man in the corner.

The pair of us were happy and excited because, at last, we were on the eve of the first day's filming for *Big Six*. Seamas and Derek greeted us with big smiles, each with a pint of Guinness in his hand.

'What are you having?' asked Seamas, shouting over a too loud rendition of *Whiskey in the Jar* from the mediocre minstrel.

Our glasses filled, we clinked them together and toasted *Big Six*. Standing in the dimly lit bar, unable to hear without shouting, we savoured the moment and got reacquainted.

The mood was relaxed and comfortable but, above all, I was totally confident the next day would give us the head start we needed. Filming proper would not begin for weeks yet. We were all working on other projects until then but because the fish were here, we had all made ourselves available.

Timing is everything in fishing and filming and we were ready to strike while the iron was still hot. I knew we were onto a winner because some weeks earlier, on my fortieth birthday, I was given an unforgettable present by our skipper.

During one of our many chats on the phone, Sean McKay generously invited me out on the *Lady Linda* for a day's pleasure fishing.

'We'll get you a big fish, for your birthday,' said the quietly spoken Ballycastle man with a strong twist of north Antrim accent.

So we sailed into the Sea of Moyle in the dark and soon after the dawn thawed the frost from his boat, Sean kept his promise. Off the chalk cliffs of Kenbane Head, lit by brilliant winter sun, I caught a 103lb male and a 155lb female Common Skate.

What a gift! In Ireland to catch any fish over 100lbs is a rare feat, but to do it twice in one day was unbelievable. Even more importantly for me, it was the best possible preparation and proof that our plan was achievable.

It was also incredible to see and to touch such big fish, caught so close to the shore. Sean didn't say a lot, but he smiled plenty that day. His professional pride at providing the fish he'd promised me, as well as the others he secured for his party, was written all over his face.

The effort of doing it was written all over mine as I played the biggest fish. Struggling with an opponent almost the same weight as yourself takes it out of you. After an hour in the shoulder harness, the back muscles cramp and it requires a considerable degree of conviction to winch them from the depths. Two fish was more than enough action for me and I spent the rest of the trip as a contented spectator.

My success also signalled part of a huge personal high for Sean, because the Ballycastle man, who works as a care assistant with elderly people in the town by night, dreams of finding monsters in the abyss by day.

He told me that years earlier, when he worked on trawl ers, he'd wanted his own boat and to run a charter service. Now, with the additional cachet of having found possibly the most prolific Common Skate fishery in Ireland, his sport fishing ambitions have been realised.

'I've always been drawn to the sea. There's just some-thing about it,' he told me.

Well, he may not be able to put his finger on what it is

that she does for him, but there's no doubt he has found the key to catching her biggest fish. And his calling was my opportunity. Sean had allowed me to clash with these Titans but without the pressure of having to do it for the camera.

As my best fish lay flat on the box covering the diesel engine, I stroked her texture, felt her alien form and marvelled at nature's precision. She was big, oddly beautiful and strangely conceived.

Her long, muscular tail was guarded on both sides by a row of sharp, off-white thorns, just like the ones on roses. There was a lot of chatter and laughter onboard, the arrival of a big fish, no matter who's caught it, always causes a stir. But while I joined in, a lot of my mind stayed with the fish.

I was struck by how much these prehistoric heavyweights look like submersible stealth bombers. That analogy with aircraft is apt because these enormous fish 'fly' underwater, using wings that have evolved from pectoral fins.

I noted how her skin on top was mid-brown with darker chocolate spots and was strangely rough to the touch. Like her close cousin, the shark, she had no scales. Instead, this species is covered in bumps and longer thorns called dermal denticles, the same stuff that their teeth are made from.

But on the underside, the skin was whitish grey and ultra slick. When I was a boy I loved drawing sharks and for me the five gill slits in front of the pectorals were just as important a feature as the teeth. It was a special treat to see and actually touch those flaps of skin arranged in a crescent. Her large, letterbox mouth was also impressive and armed with hundreds of tiny platelet teeth, used to crush food to a pulp.

These big fish are supremely adapted for a life scavenging, hunting and killing on the bottom of the sea. Her eyes were big and see ten times better than us in the dark. But they don't need to see at all to hunt. They have all the electro-receptors of the shark family, able to detect the living pulse of prey close up, even if it's hiding under sand. Two thirds of the brain is linked to scent detection and the nostrils, while linked to the respiratory system, are used solely to sniff out food.

I was mindful of that encounter and that glorious, calm day as I finished my pint. I fully expected we would repeat it the next morning as we headed back to the hotel. Battle would commence at 5.30am. I couldn't wait.

On the short journey to the fishing grounds, a golden dawn burst over Fair Head. It floodlit the white cliffs of Rathlin Island and kissed the deep blue sea. It was early, but the Atlantic Ocean was wide-awake and in a mood to play havoc with our plans.

Weeks of high winds and winter storms had pushed and pulled her surface and now she was in perpetual, chaotic motion. The effect was striking. Even so close to shore the *Lady Linda* was rolling and swaying, pitching and climbing. At the foot of the cliffs, the swells smashed hard and high.

'I didn't expect it to be just this bad,' said Sean. We'd had to stand down three previous attempts at getting out because of the weather. It was perfectly safe, the wind was light and blowing off the land but he knew a big swell is always a killer.

The anchor was dropped 240 feet and immediately the rise and fall of the bow was complicated by a side-to-side action that only the best sea legs could withstand.

The first bite came before I began to feel really ill. Sean's friend Brian Foster handed me his rod. The former Irish international angler uses a super-stiff 80lb class rod and yet it had a formidable bend in it.

He and his great friend Uel Moore, another top class fisherman who's also represented his country, were to fish with me but it was agreed I should catch the first big one. Experience told Brian I was in contact with a large male, well over the magical 100lb mark. It was pulling with the force of an ox dragging a plough.

I sat down and settled into the role of fishing presenter. What a start! I could not have been happier or more excited. We'd hit on the idea of starting a stopwatch at the beginning of the fight as a nice visual aid, a way of punctuating the action and telling the story. I remember after seven minutes beginning to explain how I was already feeling the pressure on my back.

Rather than burn hours of tape, the camera was then switched off, awaiting the next dramatic soundbite from the fool at the thick end of the rod. I couldn't get over how well it was going when suddenly it all went pear-shaped.

After twenty two minutes the huge fish at the sharp end spat the whole mackerel out. The line went limp. What had been a real life tug-o'-war with a monster more than

200 feet down was now fiction. It was the first indication that my idyllic, birthday introduction to this game would not be repeated.

The second bad sign quickly followed. I could feel the slow, light-headed and inevitable sweaty sense that the sea, as well as the fish, was having its revenge. The stiff tongue, the hot flush and spinning head were all a prelude to vomiting the half a cup of tea and an apple I'd had for breakfast.

The agony was intensified by the fact that another rod was bent in an inverted smile that usually delights the fisherman. At that moment, I was far from happy.

But the show must go on; we had a film to make. I took the slow heavy pull, sat down on the hard plastic cover of the life raft and tried to be a fishing presenter. Staring into the camera lens, like a condemned man looking down the barrel of a gun, I remember saying something to the firing squad.

'You'll have to forgive me if I'm sick during this, I'm feeling a little queasy.' It was the best I could do.

Sean has seen men fight these fish for up to three hours and not get them aboard. But this time, after an astonishingly short battle lasting only thirteen minutes, the men pulled a 95lb skate aboard.

I'd had the great fortune to hook a small female who lacked stamina but even the wee ones are impressive. I felt none of the boundless joy that usually accompanies the capture of a remarkable fish. I simply wanted to lie down with it on the grey, cold engine cover and die, or at least sleep. Instead, I babbled a description. Something about it's thorny tail, crushing mouth... all delivered on autopilot.

You can't tell on telly, but my brain had gone foggy and it was a big effort just to get the words out. My stiff tongue growing stiffer by the second, I remember thinking that I had to say something to end the sequence: say it quickly, cleanly, give it a definite finish and smile at the camera.

That done, I staggered to the galvanised rail on the gunwales and retched. The heave of the sea, the swell of the water, the salty air, I was on a spinning world that wouldn't let me off. I so wanted to lie down on the rubber matting on the deck, to drift off among the fish guts and slime. There's no dignity in seasickness.

If I didn't care, nor did Seamas. The cameraman with the constitution of an elephant, who is capable of drinking and partying all night before working at peak level in the toughest conditions all day, was feeding the fish as well.

What a mess, a pasty-faced presenter whose mind had gone missing along with his trademark enthusiasm and a cameraman whose viewfinder was the equivalent of looking straight into hell. Not the start I'd imagined.

Sean, Brian and Uel looked at each other in bewildered amusement. Seamas and I were draped over the side. Derek was not vomiting but he was pallid, mute and unable to move. Carole was fine, except that the situation was giving her a huge professional headache.

It didn't register how good the fishing was, even when another big skate announced its arrival. Seamas couldn't even pick up his camera as Brian started playing what was obviously a real heavyweight contender. Fifty-five minutes later I was still dead to the world when it was ready to come aboard.

Our director, who incidentally had been watching the drama unfold as she ate sandwiches, finally sprang into action. Putting down her polystyrene cup of leek and potato soup, she seized the little monitor linked to an underwater camera.

'Up a bit, no more to the left, no left!' she called the shots thinking Derek had bravely stepped in to save the day by moving the underwater camera on the end of the pole. Unfortunately for us, he was now an even paler wreck, struggling to keep down the breakfast he didn't have. I don't remember him saying a single word during those six hours aboard Sean McKay's boat.

No, in the confusion, our underwater cameraman was Uel, the coach fitter from Larne. And his qualifications for getting such a great job as a cameraman? He could stand up and look down without throwing up. Simple as that.

Head in hands and unable to move if my life depended on it, I watched the farce from my rollercoaster seat in the stern.

But Seamas wouldn't be beaten. He dug deep, picked up his camera and filmed the arrival of a very big fish. The boys measured the length and width and plotted it on a weight chart. It was Brian's biggest ever Common Skate, a majestic female weighing in at 181lbs.

Still glued to the bench at the back of the boat, I managed a lame 'look at the size of that!' On any other day, I'd have been positively orgasmic at our achievement. We'd managed to go out and record something that's never been captured by a film crew in Northern Ireland. But on this Sunday, 9 February 2003, our team was in serious trouble.

We didn't have a single shot of Brian fighting the fish and our plans were in a mess. As the director and producer, it was Carole's job to pull a rabbit out of a hat and no better woman. She began by getting Sean to sail back towards Ballycastle and more sheltered water.

Several pounds of lead were attached to Brian's line and lowered to the depths. With an impressive bend in his rod he began to heave that big 'fish' up from the depths – filmed by the director, who also had to prompt the presenter, who'd recovered sufficiently to stand up and open his mouth.

If Brian ever gets tired of working as a fitter, there's a job waiting for him as an actor. He gave that fish line. He pumped and wound, worked and pulled and all the time chatted in a relaxed and natural way about his passion for one of the Big Six.

'When you catch a fish you always want to catch one that little bit bigger and you're not going to catch many bigger than the Common Skate,' said our star, telling the plain and simple truth.

Looking at that fight sequence on the small screen you'd never know it was filmed afterwards, it worked a treat. In that calmer water, away from the big swell that had brought misery down on us, Seamas once again braved the demons in his viewfinder and even managed to film an interview with Sean.

Carole had put us back on track, secured the vital shots

she needed to be able to tell this story on TV and it was only lunchtime. Our first day out had been incredibly tough but because the real stars of the show, the fish, had shown up, the trip was worth it.

I was very glad to be heading for the harbour. The sun had shone on us from dawn and Rathlin Island was picked out in sharp relief against a cold, blue backcloth of sea and sky. Fair Head pointed the way to the Mull of Kintyre and it was clear to me that nothing had changed here for countless ages.

Sailing towards Ballycastle, I felt somehow smaller, more insignificant than when we left. We'd gone to sea to find creatures to fire the imagination but the reality of their world and the power of their home had humbled us.

That wicked mistress, the sea, was back on her best behaviour when we returned in search of one more fish on St Patrick's Day. There were daffodils and day-trippers along the sun-drenched seafront when we sailed out in search of leviathans.

In February, we hadn't had a second boat to film from so all the action had been confined to the narrow deck of the *Lady Linda.* That's too claustrophobic and seriously restricts the editing process. We needed more shots and on this trip the viewers would get to see the anglers on the *Lady Linda* playing the fish we caught weeks earlier.

We used the lead on the line trick to great effect and staged several other scenes, including me pretending to be sick overboard. You really can't believe what you see on TV.

The fishing turned out to be much slower. Sean is an

impressive skipper who's really cracked the code for catching Common Skate but we were entering the time of year when they just disappear for a spell. No one knows where they go or why, and in the absence of any bites, Uel, Brian, Sean and myself were left to ponder the imponderable nature of our sport.

We watched the rod tips for any hint of action. After several hours, we did indeed get the knock we wanted and after more than an hour of hard labour, I saw my fish for the first time. That great stealth bomber crashed onto the surface, kiting down the tide a long way off the stern.

As I cranked the 6/0 Senator reel, her wings skimmed the light waves.

'Just keep winding her in,' said Sean, calmly and quietly.

'Oh, wow!' I roared. 'As a fisherman, your heart is fit to burst when you see something as big and as beautiful as that.'

I was in a magical place and at a wonderful time. The sea was Caribbean blue and the North Antrim coast was bathed in soft sunshine. It irradiated the cliffs all the way back to a dazzling image of Sheep Island and Ballintoy beyond. I had a giant fish on the line, and the fact that I wasn't seasick, that I could really stand there and share with a clear head and a happy heart such a remarkable experience was one of the most satisfying moments of the series.

It took the combined strength of Sean, Brian and Uel to lift the big old girl into the boat. The ritual of measuring and tagging one of the two tiny dorsal fins on her tail was efficiently performed. The chart estimated her weight at 146lbs – that's ten stone six pounds of predatory perfection!

I spread my arms as wide as possible and said: 'To say you've caught a fish that big is usually a lie but it's bigger than that. I'm going to retire, you're just not going to catch a bigger fish than that.'

Sean is one of about seventy skippers around Ireland who tag and release skate and other members of the shark family. The details are sent to the Central Fisheries Board in Dublin and are used to help assess stock levels.

It's particularly important for the Common Skate because it is an endangered species. They have been fished and netted to extinction in the Irish Sea and around most of the British Isles, but Sean's discovery of a thriving population is great news for them and for scientists studying them.

Studies suggest these fish live in settled, resident groups and that only a few males will leave to mix the gene pool with other populations. The nearest big Common Skate 'family' is probably the one off the Mull of Kintyre, not that far from Ballycastle, so it's entirely possible they are interrelated.

In the past, when they were caught, killed and hung up on the end of piers by anglers their numbers quickly declined to zero. When the local fish were removed there were none to take their place. It happened in Belfast Lough, Strangford Lough and every coastal nook and cranny along our East Coast.

Their shape also means that juvenile skate end up in nets targeting other species. When you consider that these fish live for perhaps fifty years but mature late and have relatively few young each year, the signs are not promising.

But the work of skippers like Sean in the north and Mary Gavin-Hughes off the West Coast are helping raise awareness that these mega-fish are best put back in the water.

Mary tagged and released more shark and skate in 2002 than any skipper in Ireland. She is a fantastic angler and a great character, the only woman skipper on our island and probably in Europe. She plays the accordion and likes a dance, but she lives for her fishing.

The dark-haired mother from Mayo was born and reared on Clynish Island in Clew Bay and has several European gold fishing medals to her credit, a talent that she can trace back to when she was three years old.

'We were in a boat and I caught a sea trout,' she told me. 'I remember how the men were so excited about it. I loved it,' she said, and her blue eyes beamed like it had only been yesterday.

When we decided to fish for Common Skate in the south, the only name on all the experts' lips was that of Mary Gavin-Hughes, so I was keen to meet this exceptional angler. It was high summer when we drove down to Mayo for a hunt with Mary for more monsters.

The initial success of our trips to Ballycastle seemed a long time ago because we had been going through a torpid time since, unable to catch some of the Big Six. So it was a slightly battle-weary team that sailed out on the *Shamrock I* on a dirty day in June.

Croagh Patrick and its pilgrims were swathed in cloud and drizzle as we bounced into Clew Bay. The sea was choppy and grey, but Mary's mood was positively sunny.

'We've been catching them all right,' she told me, dressed from head to foot in bright yellow oilskins.

I watched as she sliced small fillets of mackerel and was incredulous about the tiny baits she was preparing for such big fish. At Ballycastle a whole mackerel with a fillet of rainbow trout strapped to it with cable ties was the bait of choice.

But Mary worked on quietly and confidently offering different cuts on each of the rods. I stuck with the whole mackerel, jumbo approach. I saw her withering look as I did it.

'It's not good enough just to hook on a mackerel and let it lie for hours,' she lectured me later. 'You have to keep changing, use fresh baits, keep working.'

And she did plenty of it. For hours though it didn't seem to matter what was on the line, there was no action. By late afternoon, Carole and I shared a knowing look that said: 'Here we go again, another bad day with nothing to show for it.'

I was beginning to doubt but I did think it was brave of Mary to take us on. She told me she'd failed to find Common Skate while filming with Paul Young, the personable Scotsman who presents the *Hooked on Fishing* series on Discovery Home & Leisure.

I needn't have worried though, because after a hushed conversation with George, a friend who'd come over from England to give her a helping hand, I was handed a rod with a big fish on it.

'We might have hooked the same fish. Take it easy,' she

said. Mary has an imperious way of speaking which brooks no argument. She talks in commands.

'My fish is running, Mary, is yours?' I asked.

'No, we don't have the same fish,' she said, and we knew we were going to have double the fun.

'Are you tired yet?' I bantered across to her in the stern. 'No,' came the terse response with a wicked wee smile.

Mary was obviously happy and well able to handle me as well as a long battle with a big fish.

The hydrodynamics of skate means they can force themselves down onto the seabed, forming what seems like an unbreakable suction. We were fishing over flat sand just eighty seven feet down, but neither fish was showing any sign of coming up.

Mary told me that she'd had to take the rod off an angler to wrestle his fish away from the sand.

'He'd never have done it himself,' she said, in a matter-of-fact tone. That's what you call real 'girl power'. She put it to good use again and after forty five minutes, her fish, a cracking male over 100lbs, was deposited on the deck. While it was tagged and recorded, I was still playing the biggest fish of my life.

After an hour and twenty minutes, I was still there and beginning to wonder if I'd ever see it. I was sweating heavily inside my floatation suit. The harness I was wearing didn't fit properly and my back was stiff and sore.

'Don't give up. You're Irish, don't give up,' said Mary, as we both pumped the rod and tried to get the damn thing off the bottom.

The veins on my forehead were swollen and pulsing with the effort but at last I managed to slowly raise my prize near the surface. I caught a huge flash of brilliant white colour in the green water and was shocked by the sight.

'It's enormous,' said Mary.

'Is it enormous?' I heard myself saying, struck by the enormity of the word from a woman who's well used to catching very big fish.

'Yes, it's enormous,' confirmed Mary, while I grunted and puffed.

'Keep her coming, keep her coming, wind, wind!' she ordered and I did what I was told.

Four times I hauled that great fish to the side of the boat and four times it soared away in an unstoppable race for safety on the seabed.

'I don't know how much more of this I can take,' I said to the camera. I was tired and sore. It was taking a tremendous effort but I was determined to do it. Seamas was grinning like a maniac. He was into it; there was an electrifying tension on the boat.

Mary was now more like a midwife than a skipper.

'I can see her coming, keep the pressure on, that's it Darryl, you're doing a great job,' she said, as I moaned and grunted under the burden of delivering a big baby for the camera.

She finally arrived on deck after an hour and forty minutes of labour. She was indeed massive: at just under 200lbs, a monstrously big skate.

'Yes! Well done team!' shouted my midwife.

'I don't believe it,' I said and I really didn't.

I looked at the great fish at my feet and could not take in how big it really was. She was heavier, stronger and longer than I was. What an achievement, what a fish and what a skipper. I shook hands with Mary and we hugged.

As I basked in the glory of catching a fish that has been hunting the oceans for aeons, I was genuinely filled with awe. Drenched in sweat and overcome with joy, I found myself lost in wonder.

If anglers have a Mount Everest – there on Mary's deck, I was dancing on the summit.

THE ROAD TO
DINGLE

Throughout the summer of 2003, we had the great
fortune to travel thousands of miles while making
Big Six. From Rathlin to Cork, we drove, flew and
sailed our way through the Irish countryside and around
its timeless coast. Long days were spent cruising past stone
walls in the mountains of the west, or through unremarkable towns on the road to remarkable locations. Here's just
one brief account of a single journey and the mood on the
brink of a great adventure.

A slim, wild-eyed man of uncertain age and dubious personal hygiene stood in the road. A great shock of black woolly hair poked out dully from beneath a trilby hat. It was parked at a jaunty angle completely at odds with his dark look. His eyes, hedged by thick brows, were polished coal, deep and empty.

The three-piece suit was black, circa 1970; worn shiny on the lapels from years of accumulated grime. The shirt may have been white at some stage in the dim past but it was also caked about the collar. Under the black tie, a badly stained waistcoat and a thin brown belt.

Standing there, motionless on the grey stone-chipped road he looked frozen, numb, vacant. We stared, drove past, took a wrong turn, and stared again. It could have been a slow-motion, monochrome scene from some movie. Instead, he was an old curiosity: a sad speck of humanity.

He was the only memorable sight in Kells, a drab town in County Meath, on the endless road to Dingle. Hours of driving passed in a blur. Quaint thatched cottages, 1960s shop fronts and houses painted acid yellow, milky pink or lurid green. They slipped by, soaked by sharp showers under an ink-stained sky.

The soundtrack became monotonous. The play list on the only radio station we could receive became depressingly familiar. *Girls Aloud*, Craig David and Robbie Williams, again and again and ...

There was talk of family and friends, fish in particular and life in general as Carole drove our hire car southwards.

Among the green and yellow gorse, the roadside sign announced: A Day in the Bog. We laughed loudly, wondering if it was a tourist attraction or notice of dire punishment for speeding: 'I sentence you to a day in the bog.'

We chuckled on, embracing with smiles a little milestone of relief on the N69 through north Kerry.

Sunday evening, May 11, and only now was the adventure beginning. Months of planning had put us here. Countless phone calls had been made, details arranged, scrubbed and rearranged but we were at last on our way.

Still miles to go, but we were now within striking distance of Dingle, which still seemed a mythical place, a fabled oasis in the far west.

At the end of an endless road, we took a detour. Hugging the coast we headed up into the mountains and into the Conor Pass. The pale evening sun sent shards of light through the clouds and hit the sea in a blinding flash of brilliance. It looked for all the world as if God Himself had opened the sky and might speak at any moment.

The road snaked narrower, higher. Craning my neck to see back down the mountainside, I felt that prickly skin feeling you get when you connect with a place for the first time. Below lay the horseshoe bay, blue-green ocean, snow white breakers and sand the colour of ripe barley. The view was exquisite, an Irish paradise.

Glistening rock walls cut sharply from the mountainside let our maroon Mondeo weave precariously along the now single-track road. It was speckled with red, white and blue sheep. Beyond them, over the stony shoulder, lay a huge panorama, pockmarked with tiny lakes. They mirrored the open sky like silver holes in a green and brown patchwork quilt.

In the car park at the top, overlooking Brandon Bay on one side and Dingle on the other, my pulse raced and eyes widened. Stopping long enough to commit that glorious view to memory, we headed west, back down the mountain towards the sea and the dark islands.

Dingle itself was an anti-climax. Eight hours of driving had perhaps whetted the appetite so sharply that this little picture postcard cliché couldn't satisfy it.

Funny thing was though, that even though we'd arrived, we kept going – straight out the road for Slea Head. Carole was searching for a sunset on the horizon to America.

The evening didn't disappoint. It was a stunning place. The rush of the breakers on the tiny beach and the smell of the sea air washed away the tiredness of the trip.

In the chill of the dying day, Carole and I pulled on our coats and, leaning on a dry stone wall, we looked out at the Blasket Islands and the vast Atlantic Ocean beyond. It felt like standing on the edge of the world.

We were indeed on the threshold of adventure, a rare position to be in these days. This was the last chance we'd get to stop and stare for months, so we did just that.

The voice of the ocean was hushed. On such a breathless evening, the roll and swish of the short swell melted soft and easy into the sand. The sound is exactly the same all around the world.

And as I looked down into the sparkling foam, puffs of

sand lifted like smoke against the rocks under my feet. I imagined all the fish that must be down there. I was hungry and tired but all I wanted to do was get a rod out of the boot of the car and make this place my own.

Making a cast, even with a mackerel spinner, would have been perfect. Instead I lingered, drinking in the sight, sound and smell. Carole did the same.

Tomorrow, we would film Conger eels in the aquarium and return a forty pounder to the wild from a slipway in the harbour. But standing there, at that moment, there was a quiet majesty about this place that put our plans into perspective.

We looked west in silence. Finally, with the peaches and cream sky giving way to hot orange and dark blue, it was time to go. We gave in to hunger and the threat of not being served at one of Dingle's finest seafood restaurants.

THE LIONS OF
THE LAKES

L ooking out on Lough Derg, I had time to think. There was anticipation and uncertainty in the air. The weather had closed in. A force seven gale was pushing sheets of rain horizontally across the white horses on the broad lough.

Sitting on a wet summer seat, under some ancient ruins, I scanned the water and knew it was going to be a rough, physical day for everyone. I also had a strong feeling that the fishing would be great. My guide was upbeat too. Ferdinand Heyerman's boyish grin and enthusiasm were infectious.

'It's a great day for pike fishing,' he joked, as we launched his boat on the eastern shore.

Ferdi was in good form and seemed completely unfazed about spending a bumpy day in front of camera, in search of *Esox Lucius*. I'd been deeply impressed by this tall Dutchman when we first met at Killaloe, where the River Shannon spills out of the lough on its epic journey south to Limerick.

Standing on the long stone bridge that links Counties Clare and Tipperary, the longest river in Ireland oozed black and slow under our feet. As we got acquainted, our featured fisherman revealed his sunny disposition:

'The lake has been fishing well,' he said, in the strong accent of his mother country.

'You will not catch many pike in a day but the fish you do catch will be good ones,' he said.

He was open and honest. It was music to my ears. Exposure to too many ghillies who promise great things and leave you empty-handed had made Carole and I sceptical. My sixth sense told me we had chosen the right man and on our first day out, Ferdi quickly confirmed our faith in him.

The weather was perfect: high clouds drifted across an azure sky and a warm, soft breeze brought a sparkle to the lake. From Mountshannon to Scarriff, Holy Island to the eastern bays, we went on safari. We were hunting the lions of the lakes, exploring the wilderness in T-shirts and sunglasses. I would not have traded my place for anything.

Ferdi had the measure of the place and its fish. I struggled to excite them while he caught three beauties. When he hooked a fish, I was struck by his studied silence. Concentration seemed to force him deep inside himself. It was as if he was alone in the boat, communicating with the fish down the line.

'It's about time, we were fishing for ten minutes already!' he joked. Ferdi had rejoined our world.

'Look, a prehistoric animal,' he said holding up a pristine pike of about 14lbs.

'Sixty million years old and look at the teeth, seven hundred of them,' he added, before slipping her back.

'Pike don't eat as much as people think. Some believe they eat their own weight in food every day. That's rubbish. They eat about two percent of body weight each day. If they eat 20% at one go they may not eat for another ten days. That maybe explains why it is so difficult to catch them,' he said.

As the day progressed, it turned out exactly as my guide had predicted; it wasn't easy. Ferdi covered many miles searching for the mammoth pike for which this huge lake is famed. He carries a map of the best fishing spots in his head. That knowledge is crucial because from Portumna in the north, to Killaloe in the south, Lough Derg is twenty five miles long and ten miles across at its widest.

It looked like a blank canvas to me, but Ferdi would suddenly back off the throttle, narrowing his dark eyes as he peered at the shore, plotting his bearings. Then, with practised guile, the Dutchman would flick the tiller, so that the sixteen-foot aluminium boat would start the drift in exactly the right place.

He explained that he was putting us over the underwater structure and isolated patches of potamogeton that provide perfect cover for pike. It's a broad leaf pondweed that's also known as 'pike weed' and for good reason. Find that habitat and you'll discover the green enamelled predators that lurk there. In that swaying forest, they hang suspended in the broken sunlight, invisible, virtually motionless, waiting in ambush.

'You are chasing them, trying to find them, to trigger them, to catch them. If you succeed in that, I personally feel you have succeeded in imagining what is going on under the surface, in that underwater world,' he said as we leap-frogged about the lake from one hot spot to the next.

He was reading the water like an open book. For the previous decade, Ferdi's life had slowly become woven into the fabric of that wild and beautiful place. The lake and its fish had uprooted him and his wife from their home village of Eerbeek, near Arnhem. Now, the seasons shaped his life as a professional pike guide. It showed on his mahogany hands, stained by the sun, and the white squint lines on his tanned face.

'I enjoy it so much, being out of doors, the scenery, imagining what's going on under the surface,' he spoke slowly, thoughtfully, looking into the distance. 'I couldn't do without it.' Then after a short pause: 'It's my life... I love it. I couldn't imagine not to fish, I really couldn't.'

His second fish on our first day was a master class in how to make things happen. We'd moved to a rocky area near a scrubby little island. I knew there were pike there, in the same way you know someone's watching before you see them. I called to the crew to be ready for action.

My guide was working one of his favourite jerkbaits with his usual rhythmic elegance when a hefty pike suddenly appeared behind it. The fish looked like an olive-brown ghost, a toothy apparition shadowing its prey. She was in no hurry and appeared to hang in space, moving at the same speed as the lure. The water was as clear as air and every detail of her camouflaged coat was visible through our polarising sunglasses.

Her movement displaced the water and left an oily boil in the surface tension. I held my breath but Ferdi held his nerve. He kept the lure going, then with a quick, hard stroke he knocked the rod down and halted the retrieve. The artificial fish snapped forward. Then with a lazy wobble as it lost momentum it faltered and began to fall. The pike pounced and he struck.

'Yes!' said the Dutchman and his big smile grew wider.

He had every reason to be happy. He had forced the fish to obey him. The lure looked so vulnerable as it dropped away, so helpless, that the pike couldn't resist. That was first class angling and proof that he understands his target species in a way most fishermen can't begin to comprehend.

I was hungry for that insight. I watched and listened, taking advice and trying to learn as much as I could. I was in the company of one of the best fishermen it has ever been my fortune to meet and I wanted to make it count long into the future.

I was fascinated by Ferdi's apparently effortless ability. I'd bought all the jerkbait gear two years earlier and after very limited success had gradually stopped using it. Confidence grows with success but it evaporates faster than rain on a summer street after repeated failure.

There is no other fish for Ferdi but pike and his passion for catching them has left him with an overactive imagination. He admitted he was always thinking about them, looking for an edge. I watched him make his own bulldawg lures from giant rubber worms and saw him turn wooden jerkbaits on a lathe in the shed at the back of his house in Ballina, County Tipperary.

'It's trial and error – mostly error. The first one I made was from a broom handle,' he said.

During a break in filming, he took me aside and showed me another secret weapon, specially designed for catching vegetarian pike! He produced a big washed carrot from the pocket of his jacket. He pushed a thin wire spike down the middle of it and two treble hooks, attached to it by wire traces that were then tucked into the orange flesh.

With a deft cast from the shore, the pike-mad fisherman tossed the vegetable into the waves and twitched it back.

'It works, I've caught pike on it,' he said.

'That's not fair, man. I can't catch them with lures that cost £20 each, and you're fooling them with carrots!'.

'It proves that the pattern is not so important. It is more how it is worked, how it looks to the fish,' said my guide.

He was right. I had studied his badly battered collection of jerkbaits. Most had lost nearly all their original colours.

All of them were pitted and scarred by the teeth of count-less predators. In my boxes were the beautifully lacquered versions of the same lures, ignored by pike on my home waters. Ferdi is just in a different league and so is the lake on which he's made his life.

So I looked to him to see how it was done. It took several hours before I began to feel comfortable, like the rod belonged in my hand. He showed me how to work it to make the lures mimic the death dance of an injured fish. Then after six hours, it happened: a fish seized my flipper bait and promptly let it go. My one and only chance of the day had vanished.

The fact that I hadn't caught anything made me even more determined. I knew I was in the right place, at the right time and with the right guide. What I needed was the right frame of mind.

A day later and staring out over the storm-tossed lake, I found the power of positive thought. Inside my head, I slowly repeated a mantra: 'Carpe Diem, Carpe Diem, I will seize the day, I will make it happen.'

I was looking at a lake that had produced enormous pike in the long dead past. It was the story of one such beast that had drawn us to Lough Derg in the first place. Sitting on the shore, with the rain steadily dripping off the front of my hood, I thought about that leviathan, caught back in 1862 by a local man, John Naughton.

According to a report that appeared in *The Limerick Chronicle* on May 13 that year, it was hooked off Derry Castle and took two hours to land after towing the boat around. It weighed 90 ½lbs and was 5 feet 8 inches long.

Impossible, dubious, an exaggeration? Who knows and frankly, who cares? It is an inspirational tale. The account of its capture is included in Fred Buller's bible of big fish: *The Doomsday Book of Mammoth Pike*. Naughton's fish was also responsible for me meeting the great angling historian himself.

After a lifetime spent writing about them and fishing for them, Fred is Mr Pike. I felt a bit like an apprentice, studying at the feet of a master, as we drank coffee in the Thatch Pub in Oughterard. He'd travelled down from his holiday home on the shores of Lough Mask to give me the benefit of his great wisdom.

He confirmed Lough Derg was still well worth a visit and lent his authority to our search for the fabled water-wolf.

'It's hard to be philosophical when you keep getting so close. Don't worry that you haven't caught a twenty pounder,' soothed the old gentleman, like a grandfather encouraging one of his own. 'I had trouble catching my first big fish too. It'll come,' he said.

I am no specialist pike angler, even though I love fishing for them. I spend far too much time with a fly rod in my hand (and trout on my mind) to be that. For the record though, my best fish is a respectable 19lbs 8oz. She took Ireland's favourite spinner, a copper and silver spoon, one sunny October day when I was fishing alone – something I'm doing more and more as I get older. For some, solitude equals loneliness. For me, the silence is akin to meditation.

Anyway, after coming tantalisingly close several times,

during countless hours and over many years, I knew it was foolish to imagine that I might actually catch my dream fish on camera. But I'd come within a pound of doing it while filming for *Coast to Coast*, so why not on *Big Six?* Such is the boundless optimism of a foolhardy angler. But you never know the throw that will land a monster and in the end, I nearly pulled it off on our second day with Ferdi.

We headed out into the gale, the Dutchman taking a straight course across the roughest part of the broad lough to a point where we'd seen a pike well over 20lbs the previous day. She had appeared and disappeared at such speed that we both looked at each other with that wide eyed, shocked expression reserved for the extraordinary.

'Did you see that?' I shouted. 'Yes, she was a good 25lbs,' he said.

I'd only ever seen one other fish that big. I was with Alan Broderick, another fantastic angler and a brilliant pike guide based on Lough Deravarragh in the Midlands. We were near the mouth of the River Inny and I was just beginning to work my jerkbait lure when a big girl appeared behind it. She kicked hard with her paddle of a tail and sprinted past it in a flash. Then banking hard in about eight feet of gin clear water, she rolled on her side and inspected the black and red lure.

I could see her scrutinising the strange object, assessing its edibility, as she glided effortlessly alongside. Then she kicked again, powering past it in the opposite direction. I was mesmerised by her attention. Some people put pike down as little more than vermin. They are widely regarded as stupid, greedy fish that will attack anything. That encounter proved they are far from that.

At the time my heart was in my mouth. I was terrified she might grab the lure but at the same time I was aching for her to do it. But as fast as she appeared, she was gone. I never saw her again but I won't forget her in a hurry.

Ferdi and I couldn't find our big fish and after he caught a small pike on his homemade yellow bulldawg we kept moving, searching, hunting. The fishing was slow in the big waves and in the afternoon, we retraced our path back across the lake to quieter water among more potamogeton beds. The rain had been falling relentlessly all day and it was good to get into the shelter of the trees near the rocky shore. The silence was exaggerated after being buffeted about by a howling gale.

The birds were singing as I pitched a Manta lure into the silvery calm. It was satisfying, almost hypnotic, to make it dart and glide like an injured fish. I didn't know it, but I was finally pressing the right buttons, calling the pike to investigate. Then it happened: a big pike charged in from the left and grabbed the jerkbait. She shook her hard head left then right, churning the water into foam. Then, realising she was hooked, she charged at the boat.

It happened as if in slow motion. After hours of fishing, watching, waiting, worrying, it was a shocking surprise to find myself attached to the very creature I was there to catch. The adrenalin surge rendered me speechless, except for the instinctive 'Fish, Fish!' that I shouted to alert the crew that I had managed to hook up. They didn't need the call. I was so engrossed I hadn't noticed that Ferdi was playing a pike as well. It took seconds for me to realise that my guide was skilfully, and quietly, communicating with his fish while I lost control of my speech and emotions.

'Oh, dear God! God Almighty!' I roared several times. They were the only words I could get out and earned me a mild reprimand from Carole when we were viewing the tapes later. 'You'll have to stop saying that,' she scolded. I prefer to think the Creator of such an awesome force of nature would understand my reaction.

'That makes your heart stop when they seize the lure like that. Seize the lure and seize the day!' I said, recovering my composure enough to perform for the camera.

Ferdi's fish was quickly released. It was another fit, fat pike of about 16lbs. It was also a generous, if risky, act. He could easily have slipped it into the live well in the boat, to be kept and produced alongside mine for the camera. Instead, he just dropped it back in with no fuss. Had I lost my fish though, we'd have had no prize to hold up and show the audience. It concentrated the mind wonderfully.

But I needn't have worried because this was one of those rare, perfect days where everything was just right. I picked my big beauty out by hand under the chin and slipped her into the live well to recover. The moment of truth in the weighing sling revealed she was 17lbs 10 oz. I have to say I was momentarily disappointed. She looked bigger. It wasn't my fish of dreams but I very quickly realised that really didn't matter anymore.

I was suddenly happy beyond words because I knew

she was still big enough for *Big Six*. The arbitrary nature of weights and measures and the judgements attached to them faded out of sight and mind when I looked at that magnificent fish.

Her skin looked like it was hand painted by God Himself. The unique fingerprints of Belleek cream were laid over olive. The colour yielded to the blackest green in nature on her formidable skull. The glassy eye, with its acid yellow cornea, flicked and stared back at me. Rosy striped fins rippled and undulated as her rigid form stiffened against my grasp. What a fish!

She had a small head, a sure sign she was young and growing fast. If I'd caught her in March, she'd have been perhaps 20% heavier with a bellyful of spawn and have surpassed the 20lb mark. But this was June and I had no regrets. I was cradling an impressive fish. She had announced her existence with a thundering take and a powerful fight. My hands were shaking as I returning her to the wild. I had touched her but she had also touched me.

We were at the end of a day that had started badly. The weather had been dreadful. The car towing the filming boat, a huge RIB (rigid inflatable boat) with twin 90hp outboard engines, had broken down and delayed us by two hours. It's just as well because Derek's alarm had failed him and he was late too. He'd had to drive like a maniac from another job in Carlow just to get to us.

Lunch had been a wet al fresco affair courtesy of our chef, Carole. She had grilled steak on two disposable barbecues, under twin green fishing umbrellas in a downpour, in the middle of nowhere. The hot sandwiches were washed down with cuppa soups and disbelief. We all laughed. There was nothing else to do and somehow the atmosphere and the place had an incredibly positive feeling.

Carole's multi-skilling was above and beyond the call of duty, all to give Ferdi and myself even longer to keep the crew out on the open lough in atrocious conditions, with the aim of catching fish.

It's a bizarre business. You can't control the weather or whether the fish will show up. With both against you it's miserable. The pressure is palpable, the hours unending. When the fish do appear, the relief and excitement save the day. But this day in particular was special. I was having a ball. We were in a great place, in good company and I was fishing with a master.

In hindsight, it was the one fishing trip in the entire series for which I have only happy memories. Lough Derg had cast a spell. Late that afternoon, close to the time when the filming schedule said we should have been heading back to the hotel, I had an inkling there was more magic to come. I told Carol I had a hunch there was another fish to be caught if we just gave it a few more minutes.

She was cold, wet and miserable but agreed to one last drift, one last cast.

'You have ten minutes to catch a big one,' she said. Ferdi gunned the Honda four-stroke and moved us along the shore to another, as yet unfished oasis of weed.

He had just tossed the drogues overboard, two underwater parachutes that slowed our drift down to a crawl, when I made my first cast. Unbelievably, it was met by a shocking take. I must have practically hit the fourteen pounder on the nose. It took the lure bang on cue. Sometimes you just know there is a fish waiting for you, and when it happens there's no better feeling in the world.

'This is why we fish. It's about seeing wonderful creatures like this. Phenomenal stuff,' I said.

Everyday life is all too often a steady flat line but such moments are peak experiences. Ferdi and I laughed and called it a day. We were both on a high and it felt like the boat was skipping back over the waves to the slipway. All of us were delighted at how the adventure had unfolded. It was a thrilling experience and my two days with Ferdi Heyerman will live in my memory for a lifetime.

That evening, we had a farewell drink in Larkin's pub in the hamlet of Garrykennedy. Sitting in front of the turf fire, with red hands and shiny faces, steam rose from our wet clothing. The Guinness was perfect, the craic was mighty and the quest was far from over.

BIG SICK

Sunlight cascaded down the walls of the huge sea swell. The water was so steep it looked like a mountainside. In the morning light, the salt foam gleamed and sparkled like icy ridges on a glacier.

Hurricane Fabien on the far side of the Atlantic was making herself known to us. Her power had been stored by the ocean and the Donegal shoreline was being lashed by the fallout.

I'd wedged my back against the outside cabin wall. I was sitting on a hard bench, with my knees locked out and the cleats of my wellie boot heels gripping the engine box.

The big, powerful twin diesels were roaring along,

making light of the rough road ahead. It was like being on a fairground ride but without the fun and knowing that you can get off. I glanced at Carole. Her face was white. She wore a wide-eyed expression of terror.

Up we'd go, pushed to the crest of the huge, round-topped waves. At the summit, just like a rollercoaster cranking to a virtual standstill, the *Rosguill* momentarily stalled. Then down: fast and loud. The organs levitate inside your body cavity, just like going too fast over a hill in a car. Uncomfortable is not the word.

In the trough, surrounded by sea, the only way was up again. The view back into Sheephaven Bay and Downings beach was, for a second, glorious, then gone. It was relentless. In the cockpit, our skipper Michael McVeigh held the wheel in his broad hands and judged the waves. The windscreen wipers slapped and squeaked the spray aside. His balding head occasionally bumped the roof. The bow of the sturdy Aquastar split the waves and shouldered the white water aside.

We pressed on, further and further into the unknown. It was early in the day and optimism was still alive. We were off to fish for Blue Shark, the most beautiful fish I've ever seen. Out there, in the last great, undiscovered wilderness that washes our very doorstep they were hunting, oblivious to the surface and our world.

We were steaming out into their home, a harsh and alien environment.

Just north of Horn Head we stopped to catch fresh mackerel for bait.

Soft grey-white kittiwakes soared effortlessly on the updrafts close to the mossy green cliffs. The stone texture of the cliff-face, warmed by the September sun, turned biscuit brown.

In the cold shadows, above the white breakers and the aquamarine sea, the rock face was as black as ink. Clinging to the galvanised rail on the gunwales with one hand and working our multiplier reels with the other, we dropped the feathers into the violent sea. Our skipper, a top-flight angler who has fished for and managed the Irish International team, proved his worth. He repeatedly caught mackerel while I struggled to hook even one of possibly the most stupid fish on the planet.

The writing was on the wall very early. Derek was too ill to fish – he must have been bad because our sound man is a mackerel 'specialist'. The few pints he'd consumed the night before didn't look like such a good idea now. He's usually quiet – but illness struck him mute.

'At one stage I couldn't even move me head,' he confessed later, in his distinct accent. It's a one-off mix of Dublin with a heavy splash of Bangor thrown in for good measure.

Seamas had been on the beer too but he was in fine fettle and revelling in it. The more extreme the weather, the more he liked it. It would make a good tale to tell over a pint on his next shoot. Anyway, being a conscientious objector he declined the invitation to pick up a rod and looked content with his lot.

That left Carole. She proved that she too could catch

fish. A string of silver, green-and-black striped beauties were hauled aboard. When I became too ill to unhook them – looking down on the rolling deck was a killer – our resourceful, if squeamish, producer resorted to using an onion bag as a glove to avoid touching them.

It would have been hilarious in different circumstances but here, on a relentlessly rocking sea, Michael laughed, I didn't. This was her contribution. It was a brave one at that.

The bait caught, Michael suggested we shelter in the lee of Horn Head to make the rubby dubby. Quite apart from seasickness, this evil concoction is the best reason why I may never shark fish again. Concentrated fish oil had already been poured into a barrel and mixed with bran flake at the pier.

Michael produced a blue plastic fish box with an antiquated mincing machine bolted to it. He was to grind the rusty, cast-iron wheel while I got the good job – I had to insert about two dozen seriously rancid mackerel into a hole on top. As he cranked, the fish disappeared one at a time. They then reappeared as a nauseating puree, which spilled into the fish box.

The stench was overpowering. The putrefying flesh burst. Pungent, stomach-churning gases hung in the air. 'This is Big Stink!' I said. I saw Seamas grin into his viewfinder.

The corners of my mouth turned down, the tongue stiffened and I knew vomiting was now a certainty – it was just a case of when the dam would burst.

Fresh mackerel were added and mixed into the greasy bran and oil with a long stick – if it had been a forty-foot barge pole it would still have been too short for me.

Michael grabbed handfuls of the vile stuff and dropped it into onion bags that I held wide. Mission accomplished, the bags were stacked in a barrel, to be dropped over the side on a rope when we reached the fishing grounds.

The mixture is so oily that it quells the waves and leaves a smooth stinking trail for mile after mile. Any hungry shark that crosses the scent will follow it to its source.

I washed down the deck with salt water from a red hose, trying not to admit how sick I felt. We were ship-shape and ready to head ten miles out into hell when the inevitable happened. As I ran to the gunwales the sickness came so fast I didn't get there in time. I vomited into my hands and then again and again over the side. I remembered Ballycastle and the skate fishing when I'd been sick. I thought too about the sickness during the Conger filming off Cork. I knew I was in for a day of it.

I was also embarrassed at making a mess of myself. But there was no suggestion of going back. We couldn't afford to. This was the time scheduled for shark fishing and that's what we'd do.

Michael quickly cleared a bed for me in the cabin. 'Go down there and lie on the flat of your back,' said the big man from Belfast. As someone who's still affected by sea-sickness even after years of working in the worst weather, I felt he was looking after me because he knew exactly how I felt.

It was the simple kind act of a man who been there and got the T-shirt.

'Don't open your eyes. OK? Remember, don't open your eyes for anything or you'll be sick,' he called after me as I raced down the steps and threw myself on the cold, blue simulated leather fabric.

That black hole was to become depressingly familiar on this trip.

As we powered out, the sound of the waves beating on the taut skin of the bow was deafening. I rose and fell with the boat – not always at the same time. It jarred my spine, rattled the jaw and resulted in the mother of all headaches.

My eyes were tight shut, my body was being pummelled by the elements and the sour taste of bile settled in the corners of my mouth.

It was 12.45pm when I got sick. I took no further part in the fishing until early evening.

Michael was abandoned to set up the shark rods, periodically change the rubby dubby bags and generally put the time in the best he could. It seemed a hardship for him to be almost alone. The *Rosguill* is usually filled with the chatter and excitement of anglers who've travelled from far and wide in search of the Donegal fishing experience. Instead, he was left to his own devices – Carole was prostrate on one of the engine boxes with her eyes closed. Illness had overtaken her, while Derek couldn't utter a word.

Seamas always enjoyed the quiet and found space for himself in odd corners of the boat. He said each time he found a space to sit and take in the view, Michael would find him for a chat. And so it went, hour after hour, rising and falling like a ghost ship.

About 5pm I heard a reel singing with the high pitched wail that stirs the blood and stokes the imagination. I was glued to the mattress while action stations were called on deck. Michael had raced up onto the bow and grabbed the rod as the crew began to film him.

'Fish, fish, Darryl!' came the shouts from above as I tried to pull myself up the wooden ladder steps, into the cockpit and then out onto the deck. Michael held the rod out offering it to me. 'Darryl, can you take the rod? ... No ... not a good colour...' he said, realising that I could barely stand.

So he smiled and played to the camera while I shouted the formula words of encouragement needed to inject excitement into this fishing sequence.

It wasn't a big fish but it was unbelievably fit. I took the rod briefly while Michael prepared to lasso the 30lb blue shark round the tail and haul it aboard.

We thought she was beaten but this indigo beauty still managed to tear line off the reel with a juddering, lunging pull. The rod arced sharply downwards with each plunge and I could see her frame contort and spin in the clear water.

The thick fog of seasickness lifted a little. I'd been terribly sick and yet the life on the end of the line had made the same old connection with me that it always does. She was lively at the side of the boat and it took several attempts before Michael could get the rope around her tail. Then he hoisted her high over the starboard gunwales and we cheered.

She was small as blue sharks go, but beautiful for all

that. This juvenile was deep blue, almost cobalt, painted on sandpapery skin. The counter shading on her flanks yielded to a snow-blindingly white belly.

She was the latest in a family lineage going back 400 million years – it was humbling to touch her. I felt feeble, ill and out of my depth floating on the edge of her world – a place where she reigned supreme.

What I said I don't remember – no doubt it was enough to make the sequence work but nowhere near enough to do credit to the majesty of the creature cradled in my arms.

It was close to 5.30pm when I staggered back to my bunk below. 'Don't leave on my account!' I roared as Michael suggested we should stay longer to catch a bigger blue. He was feeling the pressure. Originally we'd planned to fish for the Giant Bluefin Tuna with him. Michael is one of a select band of anglers who've landed this turbo-charged super fish.

He'd played it for two hours and had beaten the 344 pounder within sight of his Donegal home – but that triumph was now only a memory on a framed picture.

Here he had to succeed on camera. That's no mean feat. In fact experience has taught me that it's the hardest kind of fishing imaginable. You can spend days by yourself, alone with your thoughts, digging deep into your reserves of self- belief in pursuit of a big fish. In the end if it doesn't happen it's between yourself and God. But if you take witnesses in the form of a presenter, producer, cameraman and sound recordist, it's a different kettle of fish.

We have expectations and so too do the thousands of

viewers who'll witness that failure through the wee box in the corner. They don't care if everyone on board was sick as a dog for days on end. They want to be entertained, excited and swept along by the story and, crucially, by the fish. You can't make an omelette without breaking eggs, my mother would say. And you can't make fishing programmes without fish. Well you can, but they are invariably dull as ditchwater and brain-numbingly bad as a rule. It's like sex without orgasm – it misses the point.

So I lay in the dark, fighting the urge to be sick and listening to the boom and bubble of the sea on the fibreglass hull.

It sounded like the pulse of some great living machine. Its rhythm punctuated the evening and my brain. Michael was quiet on the way back to shore. It was nearly 8pm when we tied up to Downings pier. We'd done just enough to justify the day's fishing.

Carole and I reassured our guest that all we needed was another shark, even a small one, and our programme was safe. The reality though was that a big shark was obviously better. At the bar of the Beach Hotel sat the crew of the *Bonito*. They'd been sharking as well but with more success. Five blues up to just over 70lbs had been landed miles from where we'd been fishing.

An air of superiority drifted over the bar with the blue cigarette smoke. They knew how we'd done.

Professional pride and preserving a reputation as a top skipper are additional pressures in this small community. Michael had worked hard by himself to get one fish in tough circumstances. Admittedly, the *Bonito* had fared better but would only one of them been able to catch a shark with a sick presenter and three camera crew on board? We'll never know but it's not certain.

Anyway, dehydrated and ill, I picked at an evening meal and went to bed.

The following morning promised another bright, warm autumn day as we left Downings. Michael had a party of Dutch and Irish anglers up from Cork.

So we headed for Tory Island, with its bony cliffs and quaint black and white lighthouse.

The day was a hazy shade of late summer and the journey out was beautiful. Wisps of high cloud were pulled thinly across a powder blue sky. The pattern mixed with the telltale stream of jets crossing to and from America.

It was quiet out there. The sea was glassy smooth and the swell wasn't as big as the previous day. But when the engines stopped and the ocean lifted and dropped us, the roll was elevator-like. It made me ill again.

I left the anglers to it and spent the rest of the day enduring a black eternity with eyes closed. Only the drumming of the waves on the hull kept me company. We caught no shark.

The mobile phone vibrated and chimed. Bleary eyes read 7am on the lime-green screen.

'Hello.....' It was Carole. She said Michael had called and wanted to go out early. There was a short window that morning before bad weather.

'We'll leave at eight o'clock, if you can face it,' she said, clearly offering me the chance to decline the offer of another sick day at sea but knowing that it was just a nod in the direction of health and safety. We were in this up to our necks. Money was running out, we couldn't afford to lose a day. I knew it and so did she.

'No, we'll go,' I said. Carole had been ill too and I knew she and the rest of the crew didn't want to go out again either. Everyone was resigned to another queasy day.

I drew the curtains and a lump came to my throat. The trees on the edge of the car park below were being tossed about in the wind. High clouds scudded by at breakneck speed. I swore and summoned up all the courage I could muster. 'You signed up for this, dig deep, do what you have to do,' I said it to myself, out loud, as if speaking the words would make it come true.

As we steamed out past Horn Head again I was convinced I'd be back in the dark soon. But Michael was only taking us about three miles offshore.

The weather was going to close in quickly when the storms arrived and he wanted a fast run back to port. We put three rods out for blue shark and he rigged a fourth with a whole mackerel and a heavy weight to bounce along the bottom for Tope, a small coastal shark prized by sport fishermen for its power and tenacity.

The horrible swell that had reduced me to a weakling had disappeared. I was thrilled to be able to stand on deck and watch the orange, white and green balloons – willing them to submerge under the weight of a big blue shark.

Michael was tense. His reputation was on the line.

Kittiwakes wheeled and dipped around the boat, always on the lookout for scraps. And every time they flew into the fishing lines the reel screamed.

Every head and eye flashed round with a kick of adrenaline only to curse the equivalent of a practical joke. We knew this was the last gasp. There was no way we could afford the time or money it would take to come back here.

It was now or never. I believed it was possible to force a fish to take the bait by sheer will power. But I had no faith that we'd catch a blue shark. No, I believed we could catch a Tope and have no way of knowing for certain but I think that's what Michael was banking on.

'We're in Tope country,' he'd said as we began our first drift on the offshore wind. He's confident about catching these coastal sharks and has regular charters from sport fishermen keen to hook one. So I kept a close eye on the rod, bending and straightening under the strain from the weight and the moving sea.

Suddenly, it screeched, and before I knew it the line was racing off the reel in a ferocious rush.

The 20lb class rod buckled over. I raced to it and removed it from the holder.

Flashing a glance at Michael I yelled 'Will I hit it?'

'Yes!' came the frantic reply.

I thumbed the brake lever forward to tighten the drag and lifted the rod but the strike found no resistance.

'No!' said Michael, his hands instinctively cradling his forehead.

'Maybe it was stuck on the bottom,' I offered, believing

the camera was running and that missing a fish like this was too embarrassing to admit.

There was another shrill sound as the reel screamed again and we all shrieked with delight, the fish was there. It must have turned and come towards the boat after it hooked itself. That was why I hadn't felt it.

I did the business for the camera – 'powerful fish', 'ooh!', 'aah!' etc.

I was genuinely happy – or was that just huge relief? The two were getting harder to distinguish clearly.

I was fishing with light line so I had to be careful not to play the fish too hard and part company with it.

The rod bounced downwards with such force that I couldn't speak. At last, I was able to do what I love best in the world.

I was battling a shark and loving every second of it. Peering into the depths I caught sight of a white flash of belly as the fish worked to free himself.

It looked like a big one and it was. When we saw it I was amazed at its length and build. It was sandy brown across the back with dark chocolate spots on the flanks.

He was neatly lassoed and laid on deck by Michael who was now clearly delighted. A broad smile lit his face – his reputation was safe. He'd done it.

The Tope was powerful, muscular and every inch the top class predator. I'd always wanted to catch one and made a mental note that I'd do it again for real – not for the camera.

As we gathered the shots, tagged the thirty four

pounder and prepared for the release, the wind had increased to a roaring gale.

Carole held the tiny screen on which Seamas could see the view from the underwater camera mounted on a pole.

I took the fish by the tail and dorsal fin and ran to the stern. Holding his tail, the head was pushed back and forth to revive him and to give Seamas a chance to get the best shot.

I let him go back to the deep where he belonged. Michael shook my hand and smiled the smile of a relieved skipper.

For the first time since we began filming in February, Carole displayed open joy. She clenched both fists and pulled her elbows to her side. We'd pulled it out of the fire yet again.

I sat on the engine box on the way back in, braving the elements and getting a drenching from the waves that crashed onto the deck.

'I'll never do this again,' I said to myself. I meant it. The pressure of catching any fish, let alone a big one, for TV was breaking my heart.

'The emotions are too extreme,' said Carole. 'I won't do this again.'

Even Seamas was bemused: 'What other job would we be at where there's so much sitting around doing nothing for hours, then it's working flat out for a few minutes? The fish goes back and we look at each other like "did that just happen?" '

So I sat there in the storm, thankful that I'd been spared the black hole down stairs and content that I would not have to return.

The weather was atrocious. It was as if someone up above had said 'There's the fish you need, now get out of here.'

We didn't need to be told twice.

A LONG SPOON

The grey blanket of sky parted. A pale blue eye opened and the sun beamed shards of light onto the sea. It looked like a silver spotlight was shining on the water, the straw-coloured strand and the green patchwork above Ballycastle.

They call it the definitive moment, when sunlight pierces the atmosphere and streaks the air like a curtain. It felt like the definitive moment for our mission too. We had already been to Cork and failed. The heat was on.

Sailing out of the harbour, the brief sunspot disappeared. A more superstitious fisherman might have considered it an omen: he'd have been right. It was making a weak attempt to rain when the skipper broke the bad news. Plan A would have to be ditched.

We had hoped to steam a long way out, past the northern point of Rathlin Island to a mark known as The Pinnacles. It's a suitably optimistic name for an underwater mountain range populated by hungry Conger eels. Out there, they were skulking attentively among the rock chasms, ambushing life in the void.

Sadly, we would never meet them. The weather was to blame. The wind had picked up ten miles out into the Atlantic and we wouldn't be able to hold anchor in the very deep water. Our best hope of catching six-foot long eels had, I believed, been scuppered before we'd even passed the breakwater.

'Great!' I said to Carole though gritted teeth. It was getting to me. I knew a golden opportunity had gone astray. Sean McKay had been out there, checking it out for us, the day before. Anglers on his boat, the *Lady Linda*, had taken three big black serpents from the inky depths. Two of them were about 35lbs and another over 20lbs.

You can't expect to do much better than that off the Irish coast because for some reason, our waters don't attract the really big eels. To have any chance of catching one over 100lbs, the English Channel is *the* spot. It's where the world record was caught. The 133lbs 4oz eel was reeled up from a wreck off Devon in 1995.

Of the fourteen species of Conger, the European is far the biggest and they can grow to yet more frightening proportions. There are tales of 250lb eels over ten feet long being caught in trawl nets. It's proof that Conger eels don't just hide among shipwrecks. They can and do live and hunt in the open.

It's a Conger mystery why those monsters don't grace our shores. The Irish record is relatively small and has stood for a long time. It was 72lbs and caught off Valentia in 1914. It tops the list of the Irish Specimen Fish Committee who set 40lbs as the benchmark for a specimen – the target we'd set ourselves. An eel that weight is an impressive predator, longer that the average man is tall, and strong enough to put a bend in the heaviest boat rod.

They are among our most common species yet their life cycle is cloaked in secrecy. It's known that individual fish will spawn millions of eggs into the deep ocean before dying but no one has ever witnessed it. Science hasn't caught up with the Conger. Eels are emblems, symbols of nature's complexity; they allow us to wonder what else we might never know.

Catching one big enough for our purpose was, I was told, very doable. It was the only species on our list that I wasn't worried about. I should have known better, because most fishermen will probably never catch a specimen weight fish in a lifetime. I'd forgotten the golden rule: the one that says there is no such thing as a sure thing.

Weeks earlier, I'd been so excited at the prospect of catching my first Conger eel that I couldn't sleep. I woke at five o'clock and looked out on a glorious morning. Below my bedroom window, horses and rabbits were nibbling the pasture. Beyond the fields, mist drifted over the shore and blurred the lines of the estuary. It was airbrushed silver, totally still.

The conditions looked perfect. The tranquil morning would surely mean a soft day, a calm sea and battles with big beasts on the gloomy floor of the Atlantic Ocean. I couldn't wait to get started.

We were guests at Loughcarrig House, near Midleton, in east Cork - the beautifully restored Georgian home of our skipper. Brian Byrne has a deserved reputation as an excellent charter captain specialising in wreck fishing for Conger. Irish skippers generally don't anchor over sunken ships – Brian does. He even travelled to Dartmouth and spent time at sea learning to perfect the skill.

'I get a real kick out of anchoring in exactly the right place. It's technical and the pressure to get it right is immense but I like that. Ten yards one way or ten yards the other makes all the difference,' he said.

It's a lot more work but putting the boat in the correct spot, up tide of the wreck, has consistently helped his guests catch the big fish that live there. Brian has plenty of marks to choose from. Between Ballycotton and Kinsale, he has the pick of sixty five wrecks. Those ill-fated vessels that sailed the shipping lanes between Liverpool and America are now man-made reefs.

The day was alive with possibility as we sat at the period dining table at his B&B. Seamas and Derek took the pattern from their plates, along with the Full Irish. Carole and I ate the mandatory light breakfast and popped a new brand of travel sickness pills. Ten minutes later I was on my hands and knees, retching on the pier at East Ferry. Unbelievably the tablets had made me sick.

I tried to vomit quietly. Staring down at the dirty green bladderwrack on the tide line, my eyes watered. I'd been around boats all my life, been to sea many times before *Big Six* with no ill effects but here I was, still on terra firma and sick as the proverbial dog. How embarrassing!

Diesel fumes drifted up from the *Lagosta II* as Brian made the boat ready. I fought hard not to think about another bad day. It's horrible realising you are beaten before you take the first step on a long road. There was no choice and not for the first time, I remembered that I was there because I had put myself there.

I put on a brave face and greeted our guest fishermen: three fishing brothers, Dave, Liam and Mick Wrenne. To cut a long story short, we sailed fifteen miles out to a wreck and caught only a few small Conger.

'I just cannot understand it,' said Brian, who'd anchored us over an old hulk, which many times before had produced lots of Conger up to 35lbs. He worked hard all day. When I finally lost the will to live and emptied my stomach of the mineral water I'd been sipping, he even took my rod and fished himself. He couldn't make it work either. It wasn't his fault, it wasn't anybody's fault, but Brian is a professional finder of fish. He cares and his wrinkled brow declared: 'Mea culpa.'

Our guests looked anxious too. The Limerick lads had begun the day in talkative, lively form. I liked them, maybe even envied their fraternal closeness: three life-long fishing partners tied together by family and fish.

'We've had some pretty big eels up to 80lbs from the English Channel,' said Dave.

'Because we're brothers, I think it adds to it because we share all these experiences together – and the ribbing we give each other!' They all laughed.

'When you get a big Conger there's nothing like it,' Mick told me. 'I don't care what else you do, when your rod is bent, they are so powerful, it's unbelievable.'

Not today though, and after landing a few 'straps' – small and thin as the name suggests – they became quieter. They looked nervously at each other when a bite was missed. The camera intensifies pressure when fish are not being caught. The lads were feeling the weight of it.

We'd placed an on-screen bet to see who'd catch a 100lb bag of Conger first. We didn't boat anywhere near that between the four of us. It seemed a ridiculous wager on the way back to shore. I tuned in to the deep hum of the engine and fell asleep, curled in the foetal position.

This was another mess for Carole to sort out. A re-shoot is every producer's nightmare but she knew it was a must. The time, money and effort would have to be spent. Brian and the lads agreed another date weeks later. They would wear the same clothes and we'd pass it all off as just one day's relaxed and lively fishing.

I had that hanging over my head at Ballycastle. I was wondering what more horrible surprises would be sprung, while I scanned the hardy tourists making the most of their 'July Fortnight' on the drizzly beach. I removed the spine from a fresh mackerel, leaving the guts and fillets hanging from the head. I hooked on the 'flapper' and cursed.

I had invested hope in Plan A because I believed Sean McKay would have done the business for us. He'd got us the Common Skate and given the chance, I thought he'd put us over the right fish again. The Ballycastle skipper told me he'd laid a bed of chopped mackerel before he left the pinnacles, so there'd be plenty of eels in the area. It was heartbreaking to look beyond the white cliffs of Rathlin and know they were feeding more than 200 feet down but not be able to take advantage.

Plan B now felt just that, second best. Sean was already talking about other marks along the coast that might produce eels but he couldn't promise they'd be any size – in other words, Plan Z.

We didn't have far to go. A few hundred metres from the harbour we dropped anchor over the wreck of the Templemore. It helped that I was fishing with Terry Jackson, one of the best all-round anglers ever to pick up a rod. The man from Kircubbin on the Ards Peninsula is a big game hunter.

I knew Terry's name long before I met him. He has an impressive big fish pedigree with about two hundred specimen weight fish across sixteen species to his credit. His long-suffering wife told me that she and the children had put up with years of holidays in darkest Ireland, miles away from the tourist beat, because Terry was trying to improve on his personal best Dace or better his Irish record for Roach.

He lives for it: 'It's such a challenge to find a specimen

weight fish in each species. There's a massive sense of achievement when you do it. You've done your home-work, hunted down the fish, pitted your wits against it, caught the fish and it's a great feeling to see it swimming away.'

He has an uncanny knack for catching the big ones and that comforted me. As we sorted out the bait and began to fish, I gave up on the notion that I was solely responsible for finding the needle in a haystack. Terry looked relaxed as he chatted but none of us knew how this would turn out.

After a short wait, I landed a small Conger, with an utterly black back, burnished bronze flanks and liquorice fins. Another bigger one followed, exactly the same colour and with the same bright bronze eye. Where you find one eel you're sure to find more and the first fish always settles the nerves. This was a better start than I'd imagined.

Then there was life on my line again. It knocked and plucked and I imagined a dark, menacing shape dragging the shredded mackerel back to its lair sixteen metres below the boat. I heaved and the rod went into spasm as I drew the eel upwards.

'Look at the size of that!' I bellowed as it thrashed on the surface. 'It has a head on it like a bulldog!' Finally we had a fish big enough to get enthusiastic about. It was an evil looking female of about 20lbs – it's just not known why the much smaller males are not found in Irish waters.

Soon, Terry's rod was hooped and banging hard. It quickly became apparent that it might just be the fish we'd set out to catch. Minutes passed and even with considerable pressure, the joiner from County Down couldn't lift it: 'It's really fighting. It's taking line again… there she goes; she's not having any of it.'

When it hit the surface, the length and girth of Terry's fish shocked me.

'That's the biggest Conger I've ever seen,' I said, realising it was the creature that I had written off catching at the start of the day.

When the scales nudged 40lbs, it was like the eel had read the script.

'That's an enormous fish. That fish is rare, that fish is far better than average,' I said, hammering home our achievement for the armchair anglers.

'That's the girl we've been after,' Terry agreed and I couldn't help wondering what supernatural power he had over fish.

Against the odds and despite my know-it-all pessimism, he'd found a first rate fish in our second choice venue. It was the shortest, fastest fishing session we enjoyed in the entire series. Somehow, some way, Terry had saved the day. How it happened is just one more Conger mystery to add to the list.

The sea undulated, slow and easy, like a road through a bog. Under a pewter sky the *Lagosta II* rode the gentle rise and fall. Flat out at twenty knots, she roared past the distant pastel pattern of Cobh, the picturesque port in Cork Harbour. We skimmed on, far beyond the dazzling white lighthouse at Roche's Point, the engine growling, wide open.

The sea only shows where you've been, never where you are going. What lay ahead for us was anybody's guess – *déjà vu* off the south coast. The waves, spray and engine merged to make urgent, familiar music. Our skipper was racing out to a deep shipwreck, between a rock and a hard place.

We'd fish the running tide and hope for the best but everyone was apprehensive. The memory of our failure was fresh. Brian, a small, lightly built man, sat quietly at the wheel, keeping his own counsel. Carole, Scamas and Derek lost themselves in the business of making television, collecting the travel shots. The Wrenne boys and I strung the rods and found ease in the ritual of preparation.

The heavens brightened. The blemished clouds were streaked gunmetal blue then platinum and the sun broke free. The sea shimmered and the breeze warmed as we dropped oily mackerel flappers into space.

Time passed without a fish. We'd flown down from Belfast on the first available jet at 6am, dashed from Cork Airport to East Ferry and hammered out into the Atlantic just to stop, sit and wait in agony. We were no longer in control; the fish would decide our fate.

'This is no good. We'll move,' said Brian. Playing a hunch, he took us further out. We would fish the wreck of the *Carrabin*, an old steel sailing ship, sunk during the First World War. It was a brave move and yet the eels still refused to co-operate.

Two in the afternoon: zilch. Brian paid out more anchor rope to compensate for the speed of the flooding tide. It was the intelligent thing to do. He was thinking, keeping us in the right ballpark. Tension gripped us like a fist.

'I'm not happy where we're anchored,' he said, expressing the doubt that had been silently nagging him. The anchor was retrieved and half an hour later, we were fishing again. Were we marooned over a Conger desert? Carole and I looked at each other. Our telepathy shared the same thought: 'Not again.'

Brian's decision to reposition proved crucial. At three o'clock there was a sea change. It was as if a dinner bell had tolled in the deep. The eels heard it, started to feed and at last there was no stopping them. My rod tip tapped and dipped. I read a Morse Code message from out of the blue: dot, dot, dot DAAASH! And the first fish was on its way up.

Her vice jaws clamped hard on the hook as she hit the surface. She spun furiously, moving water like a wet retriever shaking its coat. The scaleless, leathery skin was a light, sandy brown, offering a clue that the eels weren't in the shipwreck, rather they were hunting over the sand outside it.

We were off and running or at least I was. Brian had given me a pirk – a cylindrical chrome weight attached to a swivel and baited hook. Not having any idea what to use myself, I took it gratefully and relied on his local knowledge and tactics. It worked a treat. The eels just kept coming to me, one after another. I was in a groove: dot, dot, dash LIFT! Every one was hooked in the lip.

It was just like ledgering for coarse fish back home. I could picture them sniffing out the bait, seizing it, gulping and turning away. Their eyesight is poor, but the sense of smell more than makes up for it. There were a lot of them on the scent trail nearly three hundred feet below, yet Liam, Dave and Mick were struggling. Initially they stuck with their own method instead of making the change. They'd had a few offers that they missed and as is so often the case, that was just enough encouragement to keep them from switching.

Mick was the first to make the move to the pirk and was soon rewarded. Dave and Liam quickly followed and then they too were in the thick of it. At one time three of us were playing big eels off the back of the boat at the same time. Hallelujah!

Terrified they would switch off as suddenly as they had started, I fished like the sea might dry up any second. Sinuous creatures were cranked up from the cold on 80lb braid and with the lever drag full on. It was heavy handed but I couldn't afford losing them in the wreckage.

There was laughter now instead of silence. Brian was in his element. No skipper can make fish feed but he'd put us on the sweet spot when they were triggered by time and tide. He'd kept his end of the bargain by using every ounce of wit and wisdom acquired over many years as a charter captain. You can't ask more.

He moved among us, unhooking eels, holding them up for the camera, weighing them and keeping score. His professionalism was being recorded on tape along with the fish. I was delighted for him.

The brothers were thrilled to be in on the action too, with the pressure of catching fish on camera gone. It took no time at all for me to sprint well past the 100lb barrier. My last fish was the heaviest of the day, an elegant five footer of 30lbs. It wasn't even five o'clock when Brian winched the anchor free and pointed the boat back the way we came.

We were all a bit shell-shocked. It felt weird that we'd done it. The fishing had been frantic and intense. I'd caught big, powerful fish and plenty of them, yet the imperative of *having* to do it, not simply wanting to do it, got in the way somehow.

Something was missing and I was puzzled by my reaction. I couldn't put my finger on it but it seemed that patience, contemplation and relaxation had all been stripped away by making a job of fishing – the very thing that anglers do to escape from their job. You need a long spoon to sup with the devil: maybe I'd sold a bit of my soul to fish, not with, but entirely *for* the camera.

There no longer seemed any room for waiting, yet that 'down time' is often the most personally productive. It is part of the game to just feel your way, chill out, to give in to the ebb and flow of time. It's a place where you can fall asleep on the flat of your back on a grassy slope, a tackle bag for a pillow. Waking in a summer breeze, with pearly cloud scudding by, you can contemplate the certainty that the world has been turning without you.

At its best, fishing is a search not just for fish, but for meaning. It is sensed rather than seen, yet when it finds you, the subtlety can take your breath away.

Years ago, long before Karen and I had children, there

were weeks when I would fish up to five days out of seven during the summer. After work, I'd speed to the water just to be there ahead of time: to sit and to watch. With the rhythm of the water and maybe a blackbird singing his heart out, the evening dripped by at a snail-pace until the rise started. It's a process that will not be hurried. The waiting was part of it, preparation for the first bright circles of silver emerging from the darkening water.

When the fishing was great, when hard-fleshed trout splashed in every seam, glide and riffle; when I could stand like a conductor in one spot and control the orchestra with my fly rod, it was heaven on earth. The river gripped my waders and squeezed – her fish did the same with my heart.

After a mad couple of hours catching Conger eels I was a long way from that. It hadn't satisfied me, hadn't touched me. There was meaning here too. It dawned on me then, that perhaps this was the price to be paid for letting one world collide with another. Something got broken in the collision. I'd lost the simplicity of the rod without the camera.

As was repeatedly the case when we eventually found success, the key emotion aboard was relief: pure, simple, unrefined relief. Brian and I looked each other in the eye and shook hands firmly and meaningfully. We'd both been up against it and come through.

'Thanks a million. You saved my bacon,' I told him.

'No, you saved mine!' He laughed it off with typical generosity.

Off the stern, the wake fizzed white, marbled green and turned a confused blue. The sea was cold, indifferent. She was washing all trace of us away. It restored perspective. I took comfort in feeling so small in her company.

X MARKS THE
SPOT

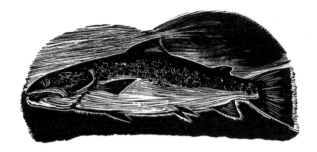

The boat pitched and rolled in a storm on Lough
Melvin on a filthy day in June. I was on my hands
and knees, the rain and waves had filled the 19ft
Angler's Fancy to the point where the wooden floorboards
were floating.

'No, No, No!' I roared at the top of my voice, close to
tears with rage and disappointment. I howled it on all
fours, with gut-wrenching, venomous ferocity.

What was the catastrophe that had left me baying like a
dog at the moon? Boat sinking? Just been sacked? Wife run
off and emptied the bank accounts? No. I'd just hooked and
lost a Ferox trout, but believe me, it felt just as bad as any of

the aforementioned scenarios. Well, at the time at least.

Carole and the crew were preparing breakfast on Maguire's Island in the middle of the lake. In the distance, I could see the plumes of blue smoke drifting into the canopy of trees before vanishing into the rain and the gale.

Their bacon and sausages were roasting on our disposable barbecues, under the now all too familiar green fishing umbrellas, when I called on the two-way radio.

'Fish! I've got a fish, I've got a fish!' I yelled into the handset. 'Come quick!'

Alastair Thorne, my fishing partner and our expert Ferox hunter, was in another boat hundreds of yards away, off Bilbury Island. We'd made the decision the previous day that fishing with two rods each in separate boats would dramatically increase our chances of encountering one of the least known fish that swim in Irish waters.

I was looking for him in the wet gloom while I carefully played what felt like a very decent trout. Down the lake, I saw the crew boat, bouncing across the waves. Our ghillie, the one and only Sean Maguire from Garrison, was at full throttle on the 15hp engine. He was charging at breakneck speed across the white horses towards me and the fish on my line.

I eased the rod higher and caught the flash of a Ferox for the first time. For the briefest second I saw the greenish hue of its silvery body, a nice fish of about 4lbs. I could also see that only one point of the treble hook had hold of a nick of skin near the chin. I was worried about it and tried to play the fish as lightly as possible. It wasn't easy though, because the boat was bucking like a bronco.

The fish was tiring and on the up-wind side of the boat. When it came to the top, rolling on its heavily spotted flank, I had to put pressure on to drag it towards the landing net. I was at full stretch with the Ferox sliding towards the net when disaster struck and the hook hold gave way.

In an instant but long enough for it to last a lifetime, I saw the fish roll slowly in the peat stained waves and disappear into the black waters of the lough. My reaction was that of many anglers when the prize is tantalisingly close but manages to escape. I sank to my knees like the wind had just been knocked out of me.

But this was a thousand times worse than losing a fish on a private trip. The experts say that trolling for Ferox can turn into a bum-numbing, brain-numbing, fishless eternity. They are seriously unpredictable, few and far between and having one for the camera, to talk about, to explain about, to adore, was always going to be a massive challenge. It was a bitter blow to lose that fish. It hurt deeply.

I'd quit howling at the lake, the fish and the absurdity of trying to command nature for TV by the time Alastair arrived. The crew had already been told the bad news and headed back to Maguire's to see if there was anything worth eating on the barbecues.

It was mid-morning and we'd been out from early. It was the second day of our two-day attempt to do the impossible. By rights we should have been trolling the deep contours of the lough in March, when most of the big Ferox are caught. But nothing is ever that easy when you are fishing for TV and where time is always at a premium. All of us were working on other projects at the time. It was a missed opportunity.

Now we were on an ill-fated trip. I had been unable to find anyone who specialised in Ferox fishing anywhere in the north of Ireland – indeed you can count on the fingers of one hand how many seriously tackle them in the whole of the island. Two of the best, John Gibbons and Basil Shields, catch monsters in Lough Corrib where they are most plentiful. But as I'll tell you later, even Basil found it almost impossible to find them when the camera was with us.

We were fishing Lough Melvin because a corner of it is in Northern Ireland. I was uneasy about it and believed we should spend all our time on Corrib, where the odds of catching the fish we needed were much better. It's all a lottery anyway and in the end we agreed to split the fishing, two days on Melvin, the same on Corrib.

With no one to call on with a local specialism, I had to find someone from further afield. I went straight to the top of the A-list. Alastair Thorne is a former British Ferox record holder with a 19lbs 10oz specimen pulled from Loch Awe in his native Scotland back in 1993.

The big sandy-haired gentleman is a fisheries scientist working out of Pitlochry where he's managed to combine his professional work with his private passion. He's also a founder member of the influential Ferox 85 group, a specimen hunting team targeting these big predatory trout.

I couldn't have picked a better man and the *Big Six* team is hugely indebted to him, not least because his research was vital to my understanding the lifestyle of these enigmatic fish. There is another reason as well. He was generous to a fault and very brave to come across to a lake he'd never fished before. He knew there was every chance he might not catch anything and that if he didn't it would be a very public failure.

Ferox are big lake trout that eat other fish and our target species in Melvin is a genetically distinct race of brown trout. DNA mapping confirms these fish are Ferox from egg till death, that they are the bigger, savage associates of the brownies. They look just like big brown trout too but there are key differences. The head is larger, the jaws more powerful and they grow bigger and live longer than standard brownies.

Their great size is down to diet, because they eat other fish. Ferox means 'ferocious' and they're well named. They'll wolf down other trout, even small pike, but Arctic Charr is the number one food item. On Corrib, where charr are now extinct, the Ferox survive on the enormous shoals of roach.

Alastair freely admits he's obsessed with these big predators. Like any angler worth his salt, he wanted answers to the big questions: How many are there? Do they have a territory? When and how do they feed?

Unlike the rest of us, he set out to get some answers. Alastair's research programme on Lochs Garry and Rannoch in the Highlands has found some of the missing pieces of the jigsaw. He's also got surprising evidence that brown trout can selectively turn into Ferox.

In Alastair's study on those two lakes, it looks like Ferox may be hybridised, that they spawned with the more common brown trout. That's totally different to the Irish experience, where they remain a distinct species because they spawn separately from the other trout.

He's been running a catch and release programme for more than a decade now and found that when Garry and Rannoch trout reach 35cms they can then turn Ferox because they are big enough to eat other fish.

And when they switch, the growth rates can be phenomenal. One trout weighed 3.8lbs when he caught it in 1994. When it was recaptured three growing seasons later, it weighed a whopping 14.4lbs. That's a 300% growth rate, but others have topped 350%.

He's also running an electronic tagging programme that has thrown up some interesting information which anglers will find enlightening.

By following their signals around the lake, he found that Ferox are not territorial. They hunt the lake in search of prey. In the evenings, he found they headed towards the shore before moving back out into the lake during the day.

Even with all his expert knowledge, and undoubted talent for catching them, Alastair also warned me that he has spent weeks at a time in the remote Scottish wilderness without catching one. That thought played on my mind as we ploughed a lonely furrow in our separate boats.

The first day had seen us troll from Garrison Bay all the way up the mouth of the Bundrowes. We trolled it all the way back again on the southern shore past the

Schoolhouse shore and on down to Rossinver.

The lake was bathed in hard, high summer sunlight and there was barely a ripple on the surface. The fishfinders pinged regularly, the small symbols denoting the black finned Sonaghan trout lying at an even six feet down.

'That's the first time they've been up this high in the water this year,' said Sean from the stern of the camera boat, a few feet away.

'I wish I had a fly rod in my hand,' I thought, but smiled back without reply.

We blanked and the pressure was now well and truly on. Twelve hours later it seemed like we were on a different lake. Perhaps the storm had wakened the Ferox in the black deeps and they were finally ready to show themselves.

I was desperate to do something to save the day but worried it might still end in ignominy. So there I sat, on my bench seat, hand on tiller, my thoughts echoed by the dreary hum of the four-horse Yamaha – hoping against hope.

The odd fish had been showing on the fish finder just before I'd hooked and lost my Ferox. There were some just off the edge of what anglers know as the Sunken Island. This shallow mound drops off quickly to about thirty feet and there are always trout around it.

Alistair and I agreed to troll its contours again. We were a long way apart when I spotted a fish on the screen. Everything underwater has a sound and I imagined a big Ferox adjusting herself in the pitch dark. She could hear the erratic, faltering procession of the lure. It drew her attention, a sick little fish irresistibly sending out the right distress signals to a hungry predator.

Her electronic image was captured at twenty seven feet on my screen and about forty seconds later the rod bent round hard and began kicking. The Ferox had pounced.

Incredible! I'd hooked another one. Again I called on the radio and again the crew came tearing out to meet me. This time there was no escape for the fish – but as is always the case, the wee ones are easy. This one was a tiddler, barely 2.5lbs and definitely not a contender for *Big Six*.

Disappointed but thankful at last to have one to talk about I insisted we featured the fish. Carole suggested we might wait and catch another, better Ferox. Experience has taught me that a fish in the hand is worth two in the lake.

Alastair put the little hen trout into a deep, black bath and added a chemical to sedate her. She quickly became limp and easy for him to hold out of the water so we could get the close-up shots that are so difficult to film when you are juggling a slippery customer.

He speculated that this speckled little fish might be up to eight years old – and at a size if it was a Ferox in say Loch Garry in Scotland, it might now begin on of those incredible growth spurts.

Sean was watching all this with a quizzical expression and then I found out why. While she was in the bath, the fish regurgitated hundreds of midge pupae and NOT the fish diet of a Ferox.

'Oh dear,' I said.

'I thought it looked like a brown trout', piped up the Garrison man over Alastair's shoulder.

'Well, it's a Ferox if we say it is,' I laughed. 'Sean, keep this to yourself,' I added. He shrugged his shoulders and smiled.

Now there was another 'big fix' in store. As the camera was nowhere near when the trout was caught, Seamas and I had to recreate the epic battle with the tiny fish. There was a plastic milk carton in the bottom of the boat that had been cut in half to serve as a baler. I took off the lure and tied my fishing line around the handle. It was then filled with water and the line allowed to spill from the reel.

I then bent into the weight of it, standing in the boat and pretending I had the little fish on the line. We knew it would work like a charm – we'd used the same trick during the filming for *Coast to Coast*.

This time too it was plain sailing and nobody could tell the difference. All this took a very long time on the rough lake and by the time we'd finished filming the capture it was time to go. Alastair had to catch his ferry home and the crew was at the end of a ten-hour shift.

'I just can't catch big fish under these conditions and with so little time to do it,' I complained to Seamas, who shared the boat ride back down the lake with me.

'No, it's not working, is it?' he said, as much to himself as me.

But it could have been worse; we did at least catch a fish. Back in the tiny harbour at Garrison I thanked Alastair and apologised, angler to angler, for having drawn him into our fishless pantomime. Carole and I drove back to Belfast in silence.

Weeks passed and as we continued filming and fishing that lost fish haunted me. At night I saw it slip away, over and over again. Carole too confessed to sleepless nights. She constantly dreamed of not catching a Ferox. She was also fretting about our chances of catching the biggest of the Big Six, the Giant Bluefin Tuna.

It felt like the entire venture was on the ropes as we headed into the west of Ireland on another Ferox hunt. I was nervous when we arrived at The Ghillie's Lair, Ardna-sillagh Lodge, near Oughterard. The home of Basil Shields looks out onto a magnificent bay on the majestic Lough Corrib.

Long telephone conversations with Basil over the weeks following the Lough Melvin debacle had eased my fears a little. I had always believed that Corrib was where the treasure was buried and I believed he had the map where X marks the spot.

I've known him for years, and known too that if anyone could deliver a Ferox under pressure it was Basil. The Fermanagh man, who spent his boyhood catching them on Lough Erne, exudes angling confidence.

He's one of the finest fly fishermen of his generation and has that special ingredient that only the best anglers possess. He understands his quarry and can make that knowledge count by putting fish in the boat.

Basil has been at this game a long time – he owned his first boat at the tender age of eight and soon afterwards started his career as a ghillie. Long experience has taught him that keeping his guests' spirits high plays a big part in having a happy boat.

'Ah well, we'll get you a fish,' said the big man from the stern, in his distinctive Fermanagh drawl. He cut a handsome figure as he stood with his hand on the tiller, a habit that makes him easy to spot at a distance when on the lake.

I needed that positive outlook. Tucked up in the bow, I was excited and anxious as we headed out onto the lake in pursuit of what had become a fabled fish.

The day was fine and bright, the sky big and blue and the prospects for success, anybody's guess. Basil looked relaxed and happy. His eyes shaded by sunglasses and light hair blowing in the wind, a slight smile played at the corner of his mouth.

It was odd to see him rig up a dead roach on a treble hook, instead of tying on one of his own flies. And in no time we were trolling the famous Corrib for its famous Ferox.

'This is a great lie for the big fellas,' said my host as we trolled northwards. Ashford Castle glinted like a little stone postage stamp in the distance.

'I call this Ferox Bay,' said Basil, playing his part to perfection for the camera.

Soon after, his rod swung round with the ferocity reserved for only the biggest fish and the line began to scream off the reel.

'There you go Darryl, that's your fish,' he said generously, offering me his rod.

Not one to look a gift horse in the mouth, I took it and began to perform, hardly daring to believe it was possible that Basil could get us a Ferox so soon, on the first morning.

'I have a fish on! I look to the sky and say thank you,' I said. 'Finding Ferox is like finding a needle in a haystack.

'It's amazing to think that I'm in contact with a surviving link with the last Ice Age.' I was in full flow and seriously happy. Maybe we could wipe the Melvin slate clean with a fabulous Ferox.

I saw a flicker of gold in the deep and suddenly the fish was clearly visible in the crystal clear water. There on the line was Esox Lucius – the only pike I ever hooked that I wasn't glad to see.

'Oh no!' bellowed Basil.

'That's no ice age survivor, that's old Esox,' I said, laughing. It took a huge effort not to swear. But I held onto my composure, knowing that we would probably have to use this sequence in the final cut of the programme if the Ferox didn't play ball.

Inside, my heart was breaking. I was laughing and acting the happy-go-lucky fisherman for the camera but that's all it was, a performance. I was struggling with that pike and the realisation that we might not be able to catch a Ferox at all.

Hours later, still trailing our dead roach over the invisible reefs below us, Basil's rod knocked and then bounced. Against the odds, it looked like the man in whom I had so much faith was actually going to do the business for us.

He was clearly excited. 'It feels like a good fish,' he said, his voice raised, a sure sign of fast beating heart. The film boat was beautifully positioned, parallel to us. Seamas was getting every detail and Derek, with his headphones on, was seated, monitoring the sound. Carole was crouched over fists clenched shut, willing the fish into the landing net.

They then recorded what none of us could bear to hear.

'Oh, no, she's gone, she's gone,' said Basil, as the life on the line disappeared.

'That's the worst kind of luck,' was the only line I could muster to fill the void.

I could have cried with frustration. It got worse too. The next day passed in a fishless trance. After two full days trolling, Basil had lost what may, or may not have been a Ferox, and I had caught a pike.

Driving north after another failed attempt, it was a long, despondent journey home.

In August, weeks later, we returned to Corrib. I was getting into the boat when I caught a look on Basil's face. His expression was that of a man who's going to work, and not work that he wanted to go to either. Minutes later he was back to his usual form, talking about the fish and fishing. I felt guilty though. Just like Alastair, I'd pulled him into an incredibly tough situation.

Two days more were spent trolling the fishless depths. At ten hours per day, multiplied by the two rods, that meant a total of forty rod hours for no fish – add to that the forty rod hours from the previous trip and the grand total was eighty.

If you'd spent eight hours a day for ten days without success, most men would give it up as a bad job and go seek the comfort of several pints of the black stuff. Basil's belief in himself and in the lake was unshakeable. He insisted it would happen but I had lost all faith.

We'd been trolling so long we ran out of things to say to each other. Manchester United and great players of the past, present and future were discussed in detail. Women, cars, jobs and family also got a turn. Competition fishing, rainbow trout, boobies and blobs, high-density fly lines... we talked ourselves to a piscatorial standstill.

We sat there, willing the lake to yield her treasure and watching the scenery and the shoreline change, hour by hour. Occasionally Basil would burst into fits of laughter.

'I can't believe this!' he'd say. 'This is unreal,' he added for emphasis and his voice carried over the stillness of the glassy lough.

It was stiflingly hot and no other fisherman with any sense was on the lake. We coughed our way through clouds of tiny green midge that had hatched by the million. We also saw shoals of brown trout cut the mirror surface with dorsal and the tip of the tail as they cruised along, filling their stomachs.

In the distance, towards Doorus, we could see enormous white splashes from fresh run salmon that had poured into the lake from the sea, miles below at Galway. The water shimmered in the heat haze and the islands looked like they were floating in air.

The beauty of the place cannot be denied, nor too could

the difficulty of catching its ice age trout. We waved good-bye on the shore, wondering when next we'd meet and would we ever be rewarded with a fish.

That night I kept an appointment with several pints of the 'black stuff' in the Thatch bar, in Oughterard. The next morning, hung over and badly slept, I began the long journey home in a fit of despondency.

I didn't have long to wait to hear from Basil. The following weekend I was pike fishing with my fishing partner Andy on a wee lake in County Monaghan when the mobile rang. Leaning against a big rock, I tossed maggots to a shoal of perch that were hunting fry in the shallows as I answered the phone.

'You should have been here today, Darryl,' said Basil, still stirred by his success.

'The Ferox have come on at last. We got two this afternoon. One of them was 16½lbs, the other a bit over 11. I had a client who wants them for a glass case, to have them stuffed and mounted. They are great fish,' he said.

Far from being pleased, I was disappointed and frustrated. Time is the best ally any fisherman can find. Time to fish, to explore, to be in the right place at the right time. Basil spends his life on the windswept wilderness in the west. It was only a matter of time until he did meet the kind of fish that we needed to catch on camera. My mood was black. 'Two fewer fish in the lake for us to catch,' I thought.

'What do you think, Basil?' I said, recovering my composure and flicking more maggots into the gin clear water. A little perch at the front shot forward and inhaled one.

'Should we make plans to come down?'

'Let me check it out this week,' came the cautious response.

We agreed that Basil would go Ferox hunting again midweek and if he caught any, we'd race down early on the next Saturday morning. The budget would now only run to one more trip to Corrib – it would be a day of reckoning.

The tension was unbearable on the way to Oughterard, the fishing capital of the west. Basil had indeed caught another small Ferox: anything under 10lbs is considered a tiddler on the great lake.

We wasted no time on arrival. The relaxed ritual of conversation and easy slide into fishing mode were quickly banished. We were here to catch a fish for the camera. That imperative drove us onto the lake, blind to the magic of the place. We were imposing Belfast pressure on a lake that's meant to wash away that type of thing.

A huge question mark hung over the boat and the day but would it be replaced by an exclamation mark?

'Where are we going?' I asked.

'Straight up the lake,' was the firm reply. Basil was under pressure too.

We trolled the same triangle between the islands near the northern shore, over and over again.

'They are here, I know they are,' he said, his brow slightly wrinkled as he stared at the rod tip. It gently bent back and forth as the roach on the end described a beautiful elliptical dance twenty five feet down. The silver flanks flicked and jerked as we slowly cruised over the rocky holes off Inishmicatreer. It was a soft September day and the lake and the conditions were perfect.

When it happened, when we found the X that marked the spot, it was a shock. In a heart-stopping instant a Ferox had lunged in the darkness and hit the roach hard from behind. The single treble hook pierced his toothy jaw and fifty yards away Basil's reel was shedding line.

My heart nearly leapt from my chest. Would it stay on? Oh please God, I thought, let it stay on.

'There he is, Darryl, there he is. We're in, we're in, we're in!' He repeated it as if confirming that it was really happening.

'I don't believe it. Is it a pike?' I asked, half joking.

'No pike this time,' said the big man standing in the boat, talking fast. He was so relieved to have caught the fish he'd promised us, that there was a quiver in this voice.

'It's a good fish, now, it's a good fish,' he said. All I could do was offer encouragement and get the net ready to receive a visitor that had taken its time arriving.

When I saw it I couldn't believe my eyes. It was without doubt the most beautiful trout I've ever seen. The skin was reflective gold – the sort of shiny brightness you get on the foil on some chocolate bars. And as it slipped into the net it was a brute. We estimated it at over 10lbs, a specimen fish, a Big Six contender at last.

'That is the most enormous fish, an aquatic leopard,' I said, overwhelmed not with joy, but with utter relief.

'I thought we'd never get him. I've never worked harder for a fish in my life. Never,' said Basil with total conviction.

Carole produced a bottle of champagne back at Basil's house but the atmosphere was strangely subdued. We were overcome with relief. All of us were just glad that Basil had taken the burden away.

We'd got away with it by the skin of our teeth. For so long the capture of that fish had been unfinished business. Now suddenly it was behind us, in the bag.

On the same stone-chipped car park where we had in the past threaded fly rods and talked about the prospects of catching brownies on mayflies, Basil and I shook hands firmly and smiled. It was sweet to be finally free of Ferox.

On the road north, that Ferox was already ancient history. Carole and I had one last Herculean task to perform ...

THE ONE THAT
GOT AWAY

Far in the distance we could see gannets wheeling and crashing into the huge swell. They were picked out like snowflakes against the navy-blue sky and slate-grey sea.

'That's where we're heading,' said our skipper, allowing himself only a hint of a smile.

Ireland's number one Bluefin Tuna fisherman is a man of few words, but when Adrian Molloy talks, you listen.

'It's going to be rough out there today, so don't move

about unless you have to, try to spread the weight evenly.'

His piercing blue eyes flashed around for confirmation that we understood. We nodded and instinctively made eye contact with each other.

'OK, let's go,' he said, opening the throttle of the *Naomh Cartha*.

It was blowing force seven from the west as we left the shelter of Horn Head – the ancient rock sentinel guarding the entrance to Sheephaven Bay in Donegal.

The 38-foot Interceptor smashed the salt water into a brilliant white pulp as she climbed and dipped her way towards the feeding frenzy ten miles out.

There had to be a massive shoal of baitfish very close to the surface to sustain the number of birds we could see. That could only mean one thing – Giant Bluefin Tuna were feeding from below, corralling them against the surface.

It almost felt like a dream. Was I really heading out into the Atlantic to hunt some of the biggest fish that swim? The sea quickly introduced a splash of reality as we pushed further out, towards the Limeburner rocks.

The waves were big. They surged upwards, lifting the boat like a cork. The troughs were so low that at the bottom all you could see was a wall of water capped by a dull overcast sky.

It was an exciting and tantalising prospect to be so close now, especially since the Bluefins had arrived weeks later than any other year. We were growing increasingly desperate for news of these big fish when word finally came though that they had arrived in large numbers off Downings in early October.

Closer and closer we drew to the carnage signalled by the chaos of diving birds.

Finally we were within striking distance of a scene that had been a dream and a nightmare for nearly two years. When we made the pitch to the suits, telling them what they could expect to see in the *Big Six*, we offered them excitement and adventure.

It was the Bluefin Tuna that we'd chosen to illustrate what it was all about: the ferocious speed of a creature that can accelerate from nought to fifty miles per hour in a heartbeat. A Formula One fish so strong that it rates among the hardest fighting sportfish in the blue planet. And, it has to be said, a fish with an unfathomable ability to examine a bait and refuse to accept it. Their sense of survival, of primitive suspicion of anything touched by human hand runs as deep as the ocean itself.

They are a daunting prospect. Catching one is said to be ten percent perspiration and ninety percent frustration. But hope and optimism are your best armour against the slings and arrows of outrageously spooky fish.

Here I was, riding the Atlantic long after the late great Zane Grey, writer of American westerns and catcher of vast fish. I was sailing on the opposite side of the ocean nearly a century after him, but I was hunting the descendants of the same Bluefins he'd tackled at the dawn of sportfishing. He and a tiny band of wealthy sports on the east coast had proved it was possible.

As I peered into my binoculars scanning the horizon for

my first glimpse of the big one, I could feel his spirit was with me. So too was that of my hero, Ernest Hemingway. The greatest writer ever to spill life onto a page really understood the big picture. He had a sense of being a small cog in an infinite wheel. I smiled and wondered what the two of them would have made of our enterprise.

Had anyone a right to expect to go fishing for one day and catch a fish that has eluded so many fishermen for so long? Well, if you don't dream big dreams, you're destined to live a small life. Hemingway and Grey knew that, they lived lives steeped in adventure, hungry for a glimpse of things most people don't know exist.

And just in case anyone gets the wrong idea, my references to two of the giants of fishing literature don't in any way suggest that I share their ability as a wordsmith. I am just a fan, and like most fishermen who think a little about what it is we do, I am only a kindred spirit.

It had taken a great deal of time, effort, worry and conviction for our team to get so close to Giant Bluefin Tuna. It had cost Carole and myself restless nights and cold sweats. I wanted to catch one for the camera so much I could almost taste it.

Now that we were here, beyond the reach of the ordinary, I was just beginning to allow myself to dare to believe we might carry it off.

Then, bang on cue, it happened. Someone threw a spanner in the works.

Adrian's radio squawked out a message none of us expected or wanted to hear. There was a boat in difficulty at the mouth of Lough Swilly, close to Fanad Head. The lifeboat was on its way but requested any boat in the area to go there to offer assistance until they arrived.

Adrian said nothing as he gently corrected our course to starboard and away from the feeding birds and fish.

There are more important things than catching fish, we knew lives could be in danger and we had to help. But it didn't make it any easier to leave what looked like our best chance of success.

Adrian gave a rueful glance over his left shoulder and pressed northwards. I was heartbroken. 'It's the curse of the Big Six,' I said to Carole as we sat on the engine box and stared at the deck.

It was then that I remember writing off our chances of ever catching a Bluefin. I had had enough. This was to be our last day of filming. We'd run out of money, the budget was all but gone and Carole looked ill with worry too.

We had what we believed were five strong programmes but, without the climax of the Bluefin, it felt as if they didn't matter. I lost all perspective and hope. It just felt like our trip was jinxed.

And yet it had started with such promise days earlier. Carole had taken the call from Michael McVeigh, with whom we'd fished for the blue shark weeks earlier.

'We've just landed a Bluefin!' roared the big Belfast man, his blood still stirred by the success. 'You've got to get up now, the tuna are here.'

A quick call to Adrian confirmed that he too was heading for Downings at 4.30am with two client fisherman the next day – a journey of seventy miles from his home port of Kilcar, near Killybegs in south Donegal.

We had been worrying that the tuna might not appear at all – a prospect that made us feel ill. As time had passed, the fish had taken on an almost mythical character.

But now, in early October, these huge open ocean fish were finally on our doorstep – now all we had to do was catch one. We knew doing that on camera was the biggest challenge we'd set ourselves in the entire series.

We left Belfast early the next day, after a major scramble by the producer to secure a cameraman and sound record-ist at short notice because Seamas and Derek were already booked.

'I can't wait to see one,' said Carole, who'd arranged with Michael to have the tuna he'd caught hung up at the harbour for us to film.

As we drove past the Rosapenna Golf Club we looked across the strand to the distant pier at Downings. There, easily visible, despite it being about half a mile away, was the carcass of a truly enormous fish.

And as we drove into the harbour, the creature became jaw-droppingly big. This was the first Giant Bluefin Tuna to be caught off Ireland in 2003. It was also my first look at a creature I'd read so much about and feared I'd never see. I devoured the fish with my eyes, like a pathologist look-ing for clues at a crime scene.

The fish was suspended by a thick blue nylon rope tied to a mini crane used by fishermen to unload their catch. It weighed 507lbs and was eight feet three inches long. The back was gunmetal blue, the flanks tarnished silver running to almost grey on the belly. The eyes were big, about the same size as a cow, yet the mouth was surprisingly small. Inside, little ivory-coloured teeth were set into the jaw in a single row.

The tail was navy-black and as slender as a scythe. Little acid-yellow finlets, as bright as daffodils, were arrayed on the top and bottom of the tail section.

We'd done well just to get here, but we had a problem. Our man, Adrian, and his guests were a long way from us. And just when it looked like we wouldn't be able to find a boat to take us out to them, Carole made it happen. She had managed to cadge a lift for us with the Irish Coastguard. By an improbable coincidence, they were in the area on an exercise and agreed to provide a large rigid inflatable boat to take us out to Adrian.

'I'd sell my granny to get them to take us out,' she told me. I believed her.

Adrian radioed us his co-ordinates and then dropped a bombshell. 'You should have been here earlier,' he said, in his soft, cultured Irish accent.

'We've caught two this morning. We just returned the second a few minutes ago.' And as the radio went silent, my heart sank. Here we were in the wrong place at the wrong time. The fishing curse that has dogged so many salmon fishing trips had struck with the tuna. 'You should have been here two days ago, or in this case, two hours ago.'

Bluefin are not to be caught like their relatives, the mackerel. Two in a day is exceptional, three would be unthinkable. I knew we were now chasing shadows.

When we finally tracked Adrian down there was more angst in store. His guests, whom he'd assured Carole would allow us on board to film, had changed their minds. They didn't want us cramping their style.

They were paying a lot of money for their sportfishing adventure and just didn't want to be inconvenienced. Carole and I looked at each other in horror and disbelief. She swore. I nearly wept.

There we were, bobbing about in a rubber boat, and denied permission to board the vessel we'd been trying to find all morning. It was turning into a farce. But true to form, Carole was not going to be beaten. Little by little, closer and closer, she got the Coastguard crew to cut the distance between us. When we were close enough to chat, she smiled and charmed and struck up a rapport with the men.

After about an hour of testing the water, she finally made her gambit:

'Look guys, is there any way we can come aboard? We'll not get in the way.' I held my breath. 'Okay,' came the reluctant response after a long pause. 'But if we catch a fish, you'll all have to get away forward into the cabin and out of the way.'

'That's fine, no problem,' she said, knowing that was just not going to happen. How could you possibly film the action under those circumstances? But the canny Carole said nothing. We all scrambled aboard.

The rest of the day was a huge anti-climax. It turned out, as I suspected, to be a fishless afternoon. The window of opportunity had opened briefly in the morning and was now closed firmly in our face.

Still, the sea was calm and the late autumn sun was warm. There's always hope when there are baits in the water, but as I sat and stared at the brightly coloured lures scudding along on the ocean surface I couldn't enjoy it.

It seemed at every turn there were too many obstacles in the way. My optimism was fading and fast. But the agony didn't end there. No, the weather was just about to deal us a cruel blow.

The storms forecast for the following day arrived as expected and kept us ashore. We stood on the now familiar cement pier at Downings. Despondency and helplessness had blown in with the rain.

Days passed and in the middle of the week, Adrian decided to steam out to Horn Head just to see if the sea was manageable. When we reached the mouth of Sheephaven Bay, he eased the throttle back. I've never seen anything like it.

The elemental power of the ocean was so clear. There was no horizon, only a wall of water. Each wave appeared to be stacked on top of another. It was like books piled precariously high in a second-hand bookshop, the sort of place where you daren't try to take one for fear of being engulfed.

Adrian's bright blue eyes scanned the watery mountain range and shook his head. 'It's impossible,' he said and, half an hour later, we were back ashore.

So the Mayday radio call seemed like the final nail in the

coffin. I have to admit that all I wanted to do was just get the hell off that bloody boat and never fish in front of a camera ever again.

'There's nothing we can do,' said Carole, joining me at the transom. Gripping the steel rails just to stay on our feet, we then stared back at where we wanted to be.

It was hopeless, or was it? An hour after the call for help, the radio again shattered the dull rhythm of the diesel engine and the rumble of wind and water. The lifeboat had reached the fishing boat. The crew were safe and incredibly our plans had also been thrown a lifeline.

Adrian turned the boat directly into the waves and set a course back to the birds and hopefully the fish. We'd lost a lot of valuable time but our skipper had the look of a man on a mission as he pushed and pulled on the throttle. He was reading the waves, accelerating and backing off as the situation demanded.

The charter belonged to Felix Hughes, an enormous English businessman with a big belly and even bigger appetite for tuna fishing. He spoke with a West Country accent and chain-smoked roll-up cigarettes. Felix's fishing partner had gone back home and this was the big man's last chance to hook a monster fish. He scanned the horizon with his binoculars as we pressed ever closer to the fishing.

Within a mile of the birds and feeding fish it became clear just how big an area the baitfish were being hemmed into. For hundreds of yards in a long line, the birds were working from above. Then we began to pick out the tuna, exploding on the surface with breathtaking speed and violence.

I was so excited I got pins and needles in my fingertips and my heart was beating much faster than normal. 'Is this possible?' I asked myself. 'Is it possible we might actually catch one of these monsters?' And all around the boat everyone was wildly pointing at the fish.

I felt privileged to be out there in the middle of one of the great natural wonders of the world. Surrounded by such drama, far from what most people will ever see in our all too short lifetimes, I had a sense of knowing my place. Compared with the strength, speed and power of those fish, we humans are little more than ants.

Ever since childhood, I've marvelled at natural history programmes featuring the great David Attenborough. The drama that was being played out in front of me was every bit as exciting, exhilarating and spellbinding as whale watching or exploring the African jungle in search of mountain gorillas.

Carole asked if I wanted to 'do a bit for the camera', to share with the viewer some sense of the scale of what we were witnessing. I couldn't wait.

'You could live all your life and never witness the power of what we are seeing here today,' I began. I was so excited at being there that my stomach was in knots. And for the first time in what seemed like ages, I loved the experience of being there – regardless of the difficulty of catching fish.

Unfortunately, we weren't there just to revel in being

close to nature, we had to influence it by hooking a tuna.

The tension was by now unbearable. Adrian worked quietly and efficiently at the stern. 'Keep it simple,' he said to himself as his fingers deftly untangled the lures at his feet. Normally he'd have rigged four of the massive reels and short powerful rods. But now only one of the 130lb class rods would be connected to the artificial squid and skimmed along on top of the waves.

He kept glancing up as he worked, fixing the course in his head and marking where the fish were moving. 'You can't just steam into them,' he said with a little edge in his voice. He was excited too. 'You've got to avoid splitting them up and you've got to get them used to the sound of the boat,' he said.

And for a long time it seemed that we stayed just out of reach of where the fish were thundering into their prey. I watched the gannets enter the water like javelins. They sent plumes of spray up behind them and, seconds later, appeared with little silvery green fish held firmly cross ways in their beaks. The fish were mechanically snapped down before the birds flapped and lifted into the wind.

Getting this on video was no easy matter. I stood behind Seamas who was having difficulty holding the camera and standing up. Filming fast-moving fish that showed for only fractions of a second in these conditions would have needed more than one camera. So I spotted for him and tried to read where the next explosion would happen. Soon it began to work and he captured their image over and over again.

Hour after hour, it continued and our wily captain kept reducing the distance between the lures and the fish. And they were shockingly big. Some were as wide around the middle as a horse and just as fast and athletic.

Adrian read my excitement and for the first time in the four or five days I'd been in his company, he allowed me into his world. 'Darryl, come and have a look at this,' he said in a conspiratorial whisper.

He led me off the deck and into the cockpit. Pointing at an orange and yellow smudge on the sonar screen, he said: 'That's a tuna, they're going under the boat. We're going to get a hit.' He said it with such utter confidence and delight that I believed him.

In this instant I saw the force that drives him. He was lit up by the chase and the challenge, driven on by the promise of doing what only a handful of skippers have managed to achieve: to catch the world's toughest sportfish in Irish waters.

I've been promised similar certainties by many anglers over the years.

Men who, when you meet them for the first time, you ask them the likelihood of being able to catch a salmon in say two evenings on a stretch of the River Drowse outside Bundoran. You explain that the time actually spent fishing will be limited because fishing for the camera eats time. Despite the warning they remain upbeat. I've learned that if the answer is 'no problem,' then get yourself another guide. There are no guarantees in fishing.

But this was different. I understood Adrian simply

wouldn't utter the words if he couldn't stand over them. The wind, tide, fish and birds had by now pushed the fodder fish within about three miles of land. We had reached the head of the baitball and were cutting across the leading fish at about forty five degrees when the impossible happened.

No one had seen the big fish surge its shoulders clear of the water and roll down hard on the rubber squid but we heard the result. Line was being sheered off the 14/0 brass reel at a terrifying rate. It sent up a mist of spray as it roared off on an earsplitting run.

For the crew and myself it was pandemonium. 'Fish, fish!' I called in disbelief and saw Seamas fighting to keep his balance and Derek, who was by now seasick and ghostly pale, struggling to stay upright.

'I don't believe it, I just don't believe it,' I said to Carole. Nor did she.

Adrian heaved the butt of the rod out of the holder in the transom and handed it to Felix, who was by now seated in the fighting chair and wearing a harness.

It was my job to keep him facing the fish, swivelling the chair as the tuna fought for its life. He was now in that place that all anglers want to be. He was fighting a big fish and for the time that he was attached to it he became a different person. The cares of the world were forgotten. He was living in the here and now. Felix's face beamed pleasure. He laughed and giggled like a child as he tapped into the reservoir of thoughts and feelings that make such experiences as powerful an opiate as any Class A drug.

'Come to Daddy,' said the big man as he heaved with impressive strength and his considerable weight. This was his third Irish Bluefin in two seasons and he seemed to have no fear of being too hard on the fish and parting company with it.

'It's not a very big fish,' he said and then the fish began to empty the spool in a slow, dogged run. 'Actually, maybe it is,' he said, laughing and heaving on the rod.

After only about half an hour of hard labour, Felix had beaten the fish. Now came the most difficult and dangerous part of the fight. In Bluefin Tuna fishing more than with almost any other species, it is the skipper who's responsible for catching the fish.

Adrian's ability to read the water, to get us close enough to ambush the fish and then to actually secure a strike had got us this far. But there was ticklish work still to do. He constantly worked the throttle to keep us ahead of the fish. If it was allowed to come too close to the boat before it was fully beaten, it might break the line on the hull.

When he judged the time was right, he pulled on heavy gloves and took hold of the fishing line. Working it arm over arm he began to draw the big fish alongside. He took care not to get the line caught around his hands, a potentially fatal miscalculation that has claimed the lives of more than one skipper. If an enormous fish decides to run and you can't let him go, there is only one place that you'll go, and that's overboard and down with him.

'It's about 300lbs,' he said as the creature rolled on its side under our gaze. It was probably the smallest tuna we'd seen all day. We had seen much bigger ones, tuna that would have measured more than ten feet and weighed over 1,000lbs.

But I didn't care. This was still a very big fish. We had done it. Against all odds, we had become the first film crew ever to record the capture of an Irish Bluefin Tuna. We could celebrate later, but now we needed to get the fish aboard, tag it, do a quick chatter for the camera to the armchair anglers at home and put it back.

Adrian used a flying gaff to retain the fish. It's a big hook which is slotted through the gill opening and out the mouth. It's attached to a rope which he wrapped around a rail and handed the end to me.

'Don't let go of that rope whatever you do,' he said. Carole was told to knock the engine in and out of gear in order to keep the rope tight on the fish and to keep water running over its gills. But because the sea was so rough, it was almost impossible for a novice to do that.

Each time we hit the trough of a wave, the rope went slack and I could see the possibility that the flying gaff might fall out.

I decided to risk seasickness by looking down and holding the rope on the other side of the rail so that I could adjust the pressure, always making sure the line was tight.

This worked well until the fish began to recover. Then, with each tail beat, my hand was knocked violently down against the hull. After a short time I had to give up on that – it was just too painful. So I went back to holding just the end that Adrian told me to.

Adrian and Felix were working to get the ramp out the stern so they could haul the fish up it and into the boat when I made a sickening discovery.

I reached down again to keep the rope tight and found no resistance. The rope was loose. The fish was gone. I instantly dropped it, knowing what had happened but unable to accept it.

I couldn't have let go quicker if it had been red hot. Panic flooded my body and brain. I felt sick to the stomach.

'Carole,' I said, feeling the sweat prickle my forehead. 'It's gone...' I was stammering. 'The, the.... the fish.... it's gone.'

My friend and colleague looked blankly at me, unable to take in what I was saying.

'The fish is gone?' she repeated in hushed tones. The shock and disbelief were written all over her face. They don't prepare you for situations like this when you enter the 'glamorous' world of television.

Carole, usually so cool and unflappable, was lost. She deals effortlessly with stroppy guests, ego-inflated present-ers and bolshy staff. She can take awkward locations, tough logistics, bad budgets and horrendous time pressure in her stride. But having to explain to the world's best tuna fisherman that the presenter has just had the worst case of the one that got away in history, defied her.

'The fish is gone?' She repeated it like an automaton.

'What's that?' said Adrian, instantly looking up from the stern. The man must have ears like a bat, or maybe the telltale look of a naughty schoolboy was all he needed to know that all was not well.

His question burst the dam. 'It's gone, Adrian. The fish is gone. I didn't do anything wrong,' I heard myself babbling wildly. 'Honest, it wasn't my fault. I just looked down and it was gone,' I said, finally lifting the flying gaff aboard and holding it up to show it contained no fish. I was looking from face to face hoping for absolution.

I got none from Seamas. He was so embarrassed he'd turned his back on the whole horrible scene. Carrying his camera like a briefcase, he shifted his gaze uncomfortably from his feet into the middle distance. Derek too was fidgety and, like me, Carole wore a guilty look. She also wanted the deck to open and swallow her.

'Felix, I'm so sorry,' I said, turning to the man who'd chartered the boat. He had generously allowed us to film his day and how had we repaid him? I'd lost his fish. It was unbearable.

'It's OK,' he said. 'It was only a little one anyway.'

'Don't worry,' Adrian chimed in. 'It has happened before and it'll happen again. You did nothing wrong.'

He smiled warmly: 'There's still a chance of another one.'

Their kindness made me feel worse. We all knew it was a mess but, in the best traditions of civilised society, we all chose to believe the lie.

It was just too much to hope for that we could get everything we wanted. The hunt for these big fish had been fraught with difficulty from the beginning. And in the end we'd done just enough to secure the project.

We had left it to late in the afternoon of the last day of

filming to do what we promised the suits we could do. The experience of seeing the wild Bluefins in their natural environment, surrounded by the seabirds, will live with me forever. It was a significant high spot on a bumpy road.

Riding back to shore for the last time, shivering in the late October evening, I vowed never again to fish for the camera. I had allowed the world of work to come in and break the fishing spell. I should have been ecstatic at achieving what we had set out to do, but instead, I couldn't wait to wash my hands of it.

Tears streamed down my cheeks and I fought hard to stop myself weeping openly as I looked at the infinite space of the Atlantic and the darkening sky. At last the tension and emotion of the adventure, the events of the day and the pressure of months of filming on the edge of what was possible had come to the surface.

It was a bitter-sweet sensation, knowing we had done what we set out to do. I wanted to hold onto the success and drama of the day but I also wanted to put distance between me and the experience.

'Be careful what you wish for, Darryl. You might just get it,' I whispered to myself.

As we raced away from the scene of our greatest fishing success I wiped away the tears and forced a hard smile. Somehow we had managed to beat the odds and film the one that got away.

'Thank you God!' I said, my eyes raised to heaven.

THE LAST WORD

A hare sprang from the long grass among the grave-
stones. He leapt clear of his bed and in the brilliant sunshine, appeared to levitate at full stretch.
In an instant, he was gone.

Far below the lush green cliff top, the sea was aquamarine. The black volcanic rock of the north Antrim coast
wore a white lace fringe and the slow irresistible swell
softly washed the shore. It pulled and teased the kelp in a
lazy, languid caress and the rhythmic pulse of the ocean
whispered in the distance.

The smell of the sea, the sound of the long grass swaying like water in the summer breeze, and the big brown

hare are still with me now – a lifetime away from that dreamy moment.

My eleven-year-old eyes snapped that hare in mid-air, like a camera. Once 'photographed' on that P7 school trip near Cushendall, it became one of the most enduring images from my childhood.

No one else saw the hare. Teachers and children were absorbed in rubbing black crayons over paper, trying to get a trace of the faint, weathered writing on the ancient tombstones in a long-disused cemetery.

Despite being surrounded by other children, I alone had heard the sudden rustle and caught the fleeting glimpse of the big brown hare – he had revealed himself only to me.

The animal and the place haunted me for years afterwards. It was a vivid little icon that refused to be forgotten. Occasionally the image would just leap into the front of my mind, and I'd see the hare, smell the sea and remember a special moment.

Years later, in my mid-twenties, I couldn't resist the temptation to return. I fully expected to see the cliff-top cemetery and the tumbled remains of the monastic settlement, exactly as I had all those years earlier. I half hoped I would even glimpse the hare.

My first look confirmed that I'd made a mistake: the charm had been broken. My heart sank at the realisation that you cannot go back to a place that no longer exists.

This couldn't be the spot. It was all too small. The towering ruins of my boyhood had been replaced. The great headstones that poked precariously from waist-high grass were gone. Even the awesome view from high over the sea was a bit of a disappointment.

It was there all right but just not how I remembered it. I felt strangely empty, like I'd lost something. It was a painful lesson to learn that it's impossible to relive the past. We get one go at it, one chance and then it's gone.

We all want to hold onto the special, transient moment, to recapture the excitement, innocence or euphoria of happy times, but it's unreasonable to think that they are any more tangible than wishes or dreams.

The ghost of the hare and the day he jumped into my life will always be with me but the meaning has changed. As a boy, I didn't know that scene would stay with me long into the life ahead that I had no inkling of.

Now, when I'm lucky enough to realise that a big moment is happening, I click it with the same 'camera'. Occasionally you just know that something special has happened and age and experience allow you to savour it, drink it deep and appreciate.

Even so, distance is sometimes required before any real sense can be made of things. I knew deep down that day with Adrian Molloy that I had seen and shared something amazing – the natural world of the Giant Bluefin Tuna in all its wonder and beauty. But I didn't know how important and positive an effect it would have on my professional life until much later.

In the short term, the events leading up to the capture of that big fish were so negative that for five months afterwards, I didn't pick up a fishing rod. I couldn't. The will to go on my usual winter forays to the solitude and chill serenity of Lough Beg on the Lower Bann had gone.

That was a real hardship. The pursuit of fish and the spiritual connections that go with it are as important to me as prayers are to the Faithful. I'm not a religious man, in the conventional go-to-church-on-Sunday way, but being out there on the water is good for the soul.

Fishing for TV was to blame and unfortunately for a short, dark period I associated what had been my deepest passion with work, stress and pressure – the very things we all go fishing to forget.

It's my nature to dwell too much on things that go wrong or that might go wrong. All the worry, agonising over whether the fish would show up, and when they did, would they bite, all of it closed in on me and took its toll by the end of filming.

But it's an ill wind that blows nobody any good, as the saying goes, and it was after that I began work on this book – without the therapy of fishing I sought solace in writing about it.

And it helped – absence does indeed make the heart grow fonder. I rediscovered the simple joy of fishing for its own sake on that four-day trip to Lough Corrib, when I went 'off the map'.

But it was another Big Brown Hare moment of pure joy that changed everything. Absolution came from an unexpected quarter: the television establishment.

I felt very much like an innocent abroad when I breezed into the Hilton Hotel on Park Lane in the heart of London on a warm evening in May 2004. Seamas, Carole and myself were with colleagues from the BBC Northern Ireland sports department. The reason we were there was because the *Big Six* tuna programme was up for a Royal Television Society Award.

Just to get a nomination is a big deal in the industry, so we were excited and deliciously on edge at the prospect of winning such a major award.

The huge ballroom was full of famous sports people. At neighbouring tables we could see the former England rugby captain, Will Carling, snooker star Ronnie O'Sullivan, the five times Olympic champion athlete Michael Johnston and more.

Under the enormous crystal chandeliers, there was a tangible sense of occasion. The top people in regional sports television were rubbing shoulders, shaking hands. The nominees at this black tie do were clearly preening themselves, preparing to collect the awards after dinner.

There was competition in their eyes and in the too relaxed, too casual posture many adopted. The television makers wanted the prize of a Royal Television Society award every bit as much as the athletes want a gold medal. It was an alien world to me, altogether too sophisticated for my tastes.

Yes, I wanted the award, but I didn't feel able to play their nonchalant game. I didn't dare dream that we could do it, but the shock of not getting it would be unbearable.

Nor did I dare drink any alcohol for fear that if we won I'd have to make an acceptance speech. I felt like a fish out of water, like someone would pinch me and the dream would be over. I kept thinking that I was a long way from Lurgan, from my roots in that bedroom with my brother, building the rod.

After dinner the awards ceremony got underway. In true Oscar fashion, the impossibly glamorous television presenter Gabby Logan introduced three clips from the nominations for the Best Regional Sports Programme. *Big Six* was the last one played on the giant screen above the stage.

Carole had sent them a short piece from the tuna programme, with me holding onto the rope with the tuna still attached to the flying gaff.

'If ever there was a big fish on the end of a line, this is it!' My voice filled the room and it felt surreal.

'This fish weighs in at around 300lbs – the toughest sportfish on the planet. When we decided we were going to fish for these, I truly wondered if we could ever actually do it.

'Well, the proof of the pudding is off Donegal, is in the wild Atlantic and there it is – amazing!'

Hundreds of pairs of hands clapped politely and I smiled a nervous smile at Carole – we shared a look that only people who've been there can recognise.

On stage the statuesque Gabby stood smiling. Then she said: 'We were well and truly hooked...'

The rest was unheard by me. I knew we'd done it but my reaction was a surprise. While Gabby praised 'the presenter's enthusiasm, the graphics and the sometimes hair-raising images,' my face was buried in my napkin on my knees.

I'd assumed the brace position, the one reserved for an air crash. In truth the world had fallen away from me. I was in free fall. When I opened my eyes and straightened up, they were filled with tears of delight and my entire body tingled with emotion. The moment was sweet beyond expression. Success is often hard to define – but in that moment I was experiencing it.

All my life I had craved that feeling and here at last was the recognition that I had played a part in something truly exceptional.

The *Big Six* team had braved hell and high water in the hunt for big fish. The announcement, the applause, the approval, vindicated the idea and our commitment. I'd left the series disenchanted, jaded, and fed up with fishing. Now none of that mattered, this moment was re-writing history.

With our theme tune booming around the enormous hall and the applause of the great and the good echoing around us, Carole and I walked past the large round dinner tables on the way to the stage.

Tracked by a spotlight and filmed by several cameras we made our way to the stage. I had completely forgotten my manners by now and was racing ahead of Carole, who hitched up her ball gown as she tried to keep up.

Marching up a wheelchair ramp at speed, I had a sudden impulse to dance, punch the air and show how happy I was. God knows what I'd have done if I'd been drinking. I heard myself say 'no, stay calm', very firmly inside my head. I walked on to collect the award from Olympic gold medal oarsman Tim Foster.

With Carole at my side we approached the lectern. The applause died down, the music stopped. With the spotlight in my eyes, I could just about make out the big circular tables and the shapes of the people down the room.

Taking a deep breath, I heard myself say to me: 'You're on', and I began to speak. I had not prepared a speech, partly because I didn't want to tempt fate but also because I'm not good with a learned script. It just seemed right that I should speak from the heart about a series that nearly broke my heart.

Still clutching my napkin and the perspex award, I thanked the RTS and our team.

'*Big Six* was a dream,' I said, my voice pitched higher than usual, my body betraying the flood of emotion that was engulfing my brain. Then I remembered a line that I wrote for this book.

'Remember this,' I said. 'If you don't dream big dreams, you'll live a small life. Here's to big lives!' And I punched the air with the award.

To what seemed like thunderous applause, we left the stage and floated back to our seats.

They give out rose-coloured spectacles with every gong. It's a fact that only those lucky enough to win can testify. Suddenly the trials of life in search of big fish looked much less stark.

This was the exception to the rule that says – never go

back to the scene of a triumph or a disaster because the best is usually diminished and the worst is always magnified.

Without the RTS award I might not have had the chance to revisit *Big Six* and rejoice in our achievement. I'll never forget the heartache and the exhilaration, the despair and the elation on the road to discovering giants in the deep. But I wouldn't change a thing.

In the end, the experience has strengthened my love affair with fishing. The greatest thing about angling is that the best is always yet to come. Every day with a rod is an adventure, a chance to slip the bonds that tie us to the here and now.

It's an open invitation to dream big dreams, to escape to a big life.

MORE BOOKS FROM THE O'BRIEN PRESS

THE SKELLIG STORY
Ancient Monastic Outpost

Des Lavelle

The past, present and future, as well as plan
animal and sea life, of Skellig Michael an
Small Skellig, from an expert who is passion
ate about these fascinating islands.

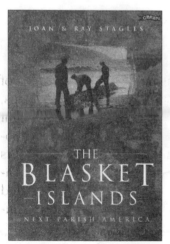

THE BLASKET ISLANDS
Next Parish America

Joan & Ray Stagles

A beautifully illustrated history of the life, tra
ditions and customs of an isolated community
that has now disappeared. Traces the fate o
the Blasket people and the slow erosion of
their culture until 1954 when the last families
were evacuated from the Great Blasket Island.

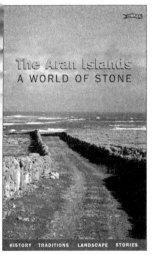

THE ARAN ISLANDS
A World of Stone

Curriculum Development Unit

An indispensable guide that explores the history, traditions, landscape and stories of Inis Mór, Inis Meáin and Inis Oírr. Highlights include the poetry of Seamus Heaney, an extract from Liam O Flaherty's *Famine* and previously unpublished photographs.

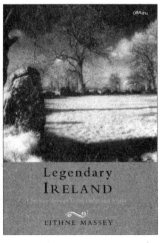

LEGENDARY IRELAND
A Journey Through Celtic Places and Myths

Eithne Massey

A journey through the places and legends of ancient Ireland – a land of warriors, queens, gods and goddesses. It visits twenty eight richly atmospheric sites and tells their mythological stories, featuring the heroic characters of Celtic lore, such as Cú Chulainn, Oisín, Diarmuid and Gráinne. Beautifully illustrated with haunting photographs and elegant engravings.

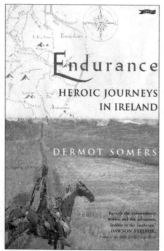

ENDURANCE
Heroic Journeys in Ireland

Dermot Somers

Mountaineer and TV presenter Dermot Somers follows in the footsteps of the epic journeys undertaken by legendary figures including Queen Medb, the Fianna, Brian Boru, Red Hugh O'Donnell, and O'Sullivan Beare, exploring the historical periods and varying landscape revealed by their amazing travels.